DEATH OF A REAL ESTATE SALESMAN

DEATH OF A REAL ESTATE SALESMAN

Jarred Kessler

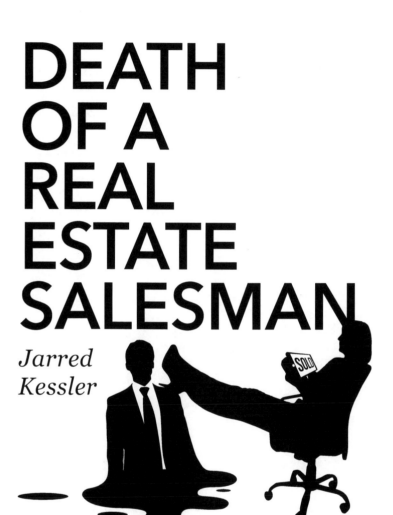

How Technology is Changing the Game of Real Estate and **EMPOWERING HOMEOWNERS**

DEATH OF A REAL ESTATE SALESMAN

*How Technology Is Changing the Game of Real
Estate and Empowering Homeowners*

ISBN   978-1-61961-614-1 *Paperback*
       978-1-61961-613-4 *Ebook*

CONTENTS

_____

ACKNOWLEDGMENTS

———

A very special thank you to my wife, Amy, who has supported and encouraged me throughout our marriage to pursue my highest of hopes and loftiest of dreams. Also, to my children, Jack and Charlie, who have inspired me to dream even bigger and make them proud. Thank you, as well, to my loving parents and supportive brother. Lastly, a heartfelt appreciation for all the people I've met along the journey of my professional and personal life, who have contributed so vitally to my entrepreneurial endeavors.

I also want to acknowledge all the dedicated professionals in the real estate community, who work hard every day and just want to make an honest living. Unfortunately, technology has a way of cutting the middle man out, and although we take a jab at the profession in this book, I truly respect and admire all the people who try to make it in such a fiercely competitive industry. I have no doubt those who are succeeding now will find a way to adjust and continue their prosperity in the future as well.

INTRODUCTION

———

A great man once said, "All things must pass." Actually, that was the title of George Harrison's iconic 1970 triple album that featured the rock classics, "My Sweet Lord" and "What Is Life?" Nonetheless, there is still great wisdom in the title of Harrison's album that can be universally applied to almost everything in modern life. Consider for a moment how so many seemingly omnipresent things in modern life have passed in recent years:

What's happened to landline telephone service in the last ten years?

How many VCRs do you see people recording television shows with these days?

When was the last time you went to Blockbuster Video to rent a movie?

What ever happened to mullets, fauxhawks, velour track-suits, wind pants, and letterman jackets?

When was the last time you walked into a restaurant and the hostess asked you, "Smoking or non?"

All those things passed—some of them for the greater good of all of humanity (especially the mullet and the smoking section at the local Denny's). This evolution of trends and functionality extends far beyond societal needs. It takes place in the business world as well—perhaps even more swiftly. For instance, think about the last time you performed any of the following actions during a normal business day:

When was the last time you heard the melodic buzzing, beeping, crunching, and screeching of a 56 Kbps modem?

How often do you flip through a Rolodex on your desk?

Do you ever conduct research without using Google anymore?

And remember fax machines? We still use them—sort of—but it's usually with an all-in-one device that prints, scans, and maybe even gives you a neck massage as it sends your document.

What's the common denominator with most of these changes, particularly with those in the business world?

It's technology, because technology drives change.

Technology is the biggest reason careers, organizations, and entire industries evolve. Take a moment to examine the way the following industries and occupations have been affected by technological change, with many of them facing possible annihilation in the near future.

Sears and Kmart never thought Amazon would be able to ship things for free within two business days.

Taxi drivers never saw ride sharing as a real threat.

Travel agents never saw Expedia, Kayak, or Trivago coming.

Investment brokers mistakenly saw the personal interaction of executing a trade as irreplaceable.

And real estate salesmen? They're all over the place still, right? That may be true as of the writing of this book, but I believe all that is about to change as well. As an industry, real estate is approximately seventeen years behind Wall Street, and it was just about seventeen years ago when online brokerage sites began changing everything in the finance industry. I should know because I spent the last fifteen years of my career there, and I saw it all happen firsthand.

MY BACKGROUND IN FINANCE

Before we get to the details of how and why the real estate market is about to go through a period of unprecedented change, I'd like to discuss a little about my background and the history of two industries that share so many characteristics: finance and real estate.

My first job out of college was not in finance or real estate. It was actually working for MTV, where I contributed creatively by writing and producing some of the broadcast content for the network. Speaking of MTV, when was the last time you saw a music video on that network? It just goes to show that, like it or not, change happens in every industry.

It didn't take long before I realized I was interested in doing something more lucrative than working on the creative side of broadcasting. That's when I left the world of music television for the much more opportunity-filled world of finance.

Originally, I got into financial services because my dad worked in finance and my mom was an entrepreneur. You could say that creative vision and an entrepreneurial spirit flowed in the family bloodlines. I've always relished the idea of creating companies that help people to save money. The idea of offering people a process that can benefit their families in the form of better vacations, more disposable income, and more intelligent purchasing power has always been an ideal I've valued.

A RUDE AWAKENING FOR THE WOLVES OF WALL STREET

My career entry into finance began in the year 2000, which was when the technological revolution really began in that industry. Since then, I've performed various high-level roles including those of vice president and executive managing director at financial institutions. I've seen a lot of financial trends come and go, and I've seen a lot of people with various personalities, approaches, and work ethics make an awful lot of money.

I had a great deal of respect for many people I worked with in finance, but many surprised me with how much money they were pulling in. These were the people, however, who foolishly thought the music was never going to stop. They were akin to the kindergartner who is left with no chair to sit on after "The Chicken Dance" *has* stopped playing during a fiercely competitive round of musical chairs.

Physically, they looked like they were straight off the movie set for *The Wolf of Wall Street*, driving a positively obnoxious, twelve-cylinder luxury car with vintage Italian-leather seats and forty-seven temperature-controlled cup holders. They consistently adorned themselves in designer suits that cost enough money to feed a starving family of five in a war-stricken, third-world nation for a year. I was genuinely surprised at how successful they were because they didn't appear to offer anything special in terms of exceptional service, brilliant strategy, or extraordinary insight. They were merely resting on industry laurels, providing some sort of invaluable service to an investor just by being there and routinely serving the role of middleman, a necessary evil in the industry. I constantly heard these people say things such as:

"This business is never going to change."

"There's always going to be the need for human involvement in commercial trading."

"The brokers have an unbreakable hold on the financial world."

"You can never replace the value of a personal interaction in this industry."

These sentiments would often be followed by boisterous laughter at the thought of innovation doing anything to change the current state of affairs or the comfort level enjoyed by all. Boy, were they in for a rude awakening! Fast-forward to today's brokerage industry, and you have a completely different landscape seventeen years later.

Rooms that were once full of brokers making phone calls and executing high-value transactions have been replaced by numerous racks of electronic equipment that allows for people to connect directly on a peer-to-peer basis. Not only does the hedge fund or other transaction get executed more quickly this way, but it does so at a significant discount to the supposedly "irreplaceable personal interaction."

In effect, the middleman in finance was replaced by the superior convenience and efficiency of direct electronic trading. Complex, but extraordinarily effective, algorithms were also created for the buy-side to connect directly with the exchanges. All the major banks came up with their own technologies to support that, but perhaps none of them were as popular as IEX, which was featured in Michael Lewis's latest book, *Flash Boys: A Wall Street Revolt.*

As a result of these advances in technology, commissions have been cut, and cut, and cut again to somewhere around 90 percent over the last ten to fifteen years. Suddenly, the wolves of Wall Street were left howling at the moon from the moon roof of a ten-year-old Toyota Camry instead of a brand-new, limited-edition Bentley.

INDUSTRY PARALLELS

That eye-opening experience in the world of finance provided me with a very unique perspective. It equipped me with the ability to spot the parallels in today's residential real estate market. Similar technological advances have recently taken place in that industry, and the arrogance of most of its agents parallels that of the finance world.

The two industries appear strikingly similar, just twenty years removed. The faux expertise of Wall Street's coattail riders was eventually replaced with fear, uncertainty, and ultimately unemployment for many. Based on recent technological trends, I can see residential real estate agents about to go through the same frightening transition.

Every industry becomes affected by technology. It's not just finance and real estate. Robotics have drastically changed the way warehousing operates. Look no further than Amazon's world-class distribution system to see that in full effect.

The changeover from a copper telephone network to fiber optics and broadband communication systems has forever altered the landscape of the telecom industry, and the list of other industries affected by technology goes on much further.

It's not a matter of *if* but *when* technology will change an industry. Part of this is because technology plays such a large and influential role in the lives of everyone today.

HEY, SIRI

All those born in the last thirty years have become accustomed to having a smartphone virtually tethered to their thumbs for constant information acquisition. People used to chitchat with each other at the train station and in the waiting rooms of doctors' offices, but now they're checking e-mail and reading their Twitter feeds.

Previous generations—baby boomers, Gen Xers, and definitely the greatest generation of World War II—valued human interaction perhaps above all else. People flew in for business meetings just so they could speak face-to-face and partake in a firm handshake to seal the deal. Shoppers flocked to the aisles of Best Buy and Sears, not only to physically touch the products they were about to purchase but also to speak with an associate about the many wondrous benefits of such products. They seemed to enjoy hearing about how their lives would be changed immeasurably for the better by purchasing something like an Electrolux vacuum cleaner.

Millennials are different. This generation is defined as anyone born after 1982. Most of them grew up with a seemingly inherent knowledge of technology, and had cell phones by the time they reached high school. In my professional experience, working with this generation involves embracing technology rather than stressing the perceived value of interpersonal relationships.

Whether you're a stock broker, real estate agent, or residential plumber, this generation, generally, prefers texting you over having an actual conversation with you. They also seem to distrust the middleman when they are involved in any high-dollar transaction. Maybe their attitude is inherited from previous generations' feeling financially exploited by some of these intermediaries. I'm not sure, but distrust definitely seems to be at the core of millennials' preference for technology over conversation, and who can really blame them?

PEER-TO-PEER POWER

It may seem as if technology has already made its impact on the real estate market with websites such as Redfin, Zillow, Trulia, and Realtor.com. But those sites empower the agent more than the homeowner or prospective buyer. All they really do is make an agent's job easier by providing a central location for consumers to find properties on their own and then contact the listing agent whose information is conveniently provided on a property's details page.

MISCONCEPTION 1: ZILLOW, TRULIA, AND REDFIN ARE THERE TO EMPOWER CONSUMERS

Wrong. The reality is that their revenues come from the real estate agent industry. Therefore, these websites only serve to further empower the agents.

The biggest problem with these sites is that their revenues come from the brokerage industry, so that's who their client is, not the consumer. Almost 100 percent of the revenue for these websites is based on advertising or lead generation from the agents, so that's whom they serve, which puts them at odds (more on this later in the book) with the competing agenda of the homeowner or prospective buyer.

What's really needed is an online platform that will support and empower the homeowner and the buyer, *not the middleman*. It's the next step in the evolution of the real estate industry, which is to allow people to execute this fairly simple, straightforward process on their own without having to pay exorbitant commissions to an agent for very little actual work. Technology is pushing the middleman out of several areas of consumer need and encouraging peer-to-peer relationships all over the global economy. Just consider the following industries where it's already happened:

Airbnb empowers people to operate their homes like hotels.

Uber empowers people to operate their cars like taxis.

Amazon empowers people to own their own stores.

So, homeowners should be empowered to sell their own homes.

Business is obviously trending away from the usage of middlemen. Their function has become nothing more than a peculiar evolutionary holdover—business's version of a human appendix. Doesn't it make sense that the real estate industry will follow suit? In fact, we're already seeing this shift. Agents used to provide three key areas of professional assistance to buyers and sellers: market exposure, transaction knowledge, and mediation assistance. Better online real estate platforms and unprecedented advances in artificial intelligence (AI) are currently evolving to render those three areas completely unnecessary.

Given these changes, doesn't it make sense to you that the biggest brokerage company in the world soon won't own a single broker?

The technological winds of change are in the air for the real estate industry, and the layperson with property to sell or a dream home to buy will benefit greatly from it. In this book, I'll show you how to leverage those emerging technologies for buying and selling a home—sans middleman—and on your own terms, saving you thousands of dollars in the process.

Exorbitant commissions and the competing agendas of brokers are about to be replaced by the convenience of peer-to-peer relationships, and transaction transparency achieved through advanced analytics and a simple, intuitive user interface. This rising real estate revolution, inspired by technology and fueled by consumer dissatisfaction, is also why we are about to witness the passing of an industry icon: *the death of the real estate salesman.*

PART 1

THE HISTORY OF REAL ESTATE TRANSACTIONS

Chapter 1

WHAT YOU NEED TO KNOW ABOUT REAL ESTATE AGENTS

———

Why do you think people have such a distaste for the real estate agent?

What is it about the profession that instills a lack of trust?

Why is there a need for a better system that cuts out the middleman?

To answer these questions, I created a persona named George Cahill, who represents your typical American male in his mid-to-late fifties. He earns an honest, middle-income living of around $50,000 annually as the sole proprietor of a custom-engraving shop in the downtown area of Dayton, Ohio. He is married and has two beautiful, smart children. One is fresh out of college and supporting herself, and the other has only one year of tuition left before she does the same.

THE REAL ESTATE AGENT'S COMPETING AGENDA

With a big house to maintain and no more kids to fill it with their clutter, George and his wife agreed to downsize and move into a smaller, more manageable home. As a fairly self-sufficient working-class guy, George decided to save some money by listing the house himself. In other words, he went with the for-sale-by-owner (FSBO) route. Within two days of placing the FSBO sign on his front lawn, and placing ads on Craigslist and other FSBO websites, George immediately became inundated with calls from real estate agents all over the area trying to secure his listing. Not one potential buyer called him. Instead, he was harassed day and night by real estate agents seeking a 5 percent commission for their *expertise* in *helping* George sell his home.

Exasperated by the agent bombardment and the lack of interest from any serious prospective buyers, George begrudgingly agreed to sign a contract with an agent. The agent did a typically adequate job of researching all the necessary comparisons in the neighborhood, and came up with a listing price of $400,000 for George's home. Within a week, he ended up selling the house for $350,000. That scenario plays out across the United States every day.

George's biggest problem with that result was that time was not a concern for him. He didn't *need* to sell right away. There was no pending divorce or job-loss situation that created a financial urgency of any kind. He just wanted to downsize and needed an outcome that was quite the opposite of the result he got from a speedy sale: he wanted to get as much for his home as possible to put more away for retirement living in his newly acquired, smaller, and more manageable condo.

THEY PUMP UP THE VOLUME, NOT THE PRICE

Worst of all, George noticed that two other similarly shaped but slightly smaller houses in his neighborhood hit the market two weeks later. One of them sold for $375,000 and the other sold for $400,000. What occurred to him at that moment was that the agent hadn't considered the fact that George wasn't in any rush to move; he was far more interested in getting the best price for his house than in selling it quickly. However, George's goal conflicted with the best interest of his agent, who just wanted to sell George's property as quickly as possible so he could move on to the next sale for another large commission.

This fairly typical scenario speaks to the competing agendas in the traditional model for buying and selling real estate, which make it such a flawed system. Realtors are always more inclined to pump up volume more than price because it's much more financially beneficial for them to sell more properties faster than to get an extra $100 or so out of one commission.

In the end, George paid his agent a total of 6 percent. He realized that if he had been able to pull it off on his own, he probably would have made enough extra money to go on a luxury vacation with his wife every year for the next ten years, and then some. Let's look at the figures for a closer examination of that reality:

FIVE PERCENT IS A VERY BIG DEAL!

Five percent of $350,000 is $17,500. Now add that potential $25,000–$50,000 that George lost because the realtor wanted to get the deal done quickly rather than waiting for the best price, and you've got a grand total of somewhere between $42,500 and $67,500 that George lost because he used an agent who had a competing agenda.

On an even smaller scale, let's say that waiting an extra two weeks would have netted George only an extra $10,000 on the sale instead of $25,000–$50,000. That still makes a big difference for him, but almost no difference for the agent. In reality, the agent splits that 5 percent commission with the buyer's agent, and half of that goes to the listing office, which means the homeowner's realtor nets only a total of an additional $125 if he waits an extra two weeks for the sale. Does that seem worth it to the realtor? Of course not. But is it worth it to the homeowner? Of course it is.

Numbers like that get overlooked all the time in real estate transactions because 5 percent here and there, along with $25,000 off the listing price, doesn't seem like a big deal when you're talking about a sale of $400,000, but it definitely is. It's real money that gets lost in the big picture, and agents have been taking advantage for decades of the homeowner's willingness to overlook it.

Therefore, agents don't try very hard to get you the best price, because they're often not likely to gain much of a financial benefit from doing so. For agents, it's really all about volume. Of course, the one exception to this is the high-end realtors such as the ones featured in the television show *Million Dollar Listing New York*. Those realtors are very willing to try to get the best price for their clients because instead of attempting to negotiate an extra $10,000, they are aiming at an extra million or two, which certainly *is* a big difference. Chances are, however, that you're not in that very exclusive market.

MISCONCEPTION 2: THE AGENT IS FIGHTING FOR YOU TO GET THE HIGHEST PRICE POSSIBLE

Not true. The reality is that agents are trying to get the deal done as quickly as possible so they can collect as many overpriced commissions in as short a time frame as possible. For the agent, it's all about volume. For the homeowner, it could be about anything. It's a natural dysfunction of competing agendas.

REAL COLLUSION

That typically horrific realty experience also involves other people jumping in on the act, forming an industry-wide level of collusion that has a negative impact on buyers as well. Inspectors, lawyers, and others all recommended by the agent share the same agenda that competes with the buyer's agenda. They're afraid to voice any concern that might risk blowing up the deal, which of course would be career suicide. In other words, an inspector is unlikely to voice concerns over rotting wood, a leaky roof, or plumbing problems if it might sour the deal. A title company might not look into a possible shortage of escrow money at the time of closing if that could delay the transaction.

Agents need the deal to go through quickly if they're to maximize their earnings potential, and they're unlikely to recommend an inspector, a title company, or other professionals who could jeopardize that goal.

LEVERAGING LIES

One of the most notable untruths that real estate agents like to tell is that buyers shouldn't worry about the commission, because the owner pays it. My answer to that: Not really. Technically, the 4–6 percent is paid by the seller to the agent, but it is buyers who actually pay it because if sellers don't use an agent, they can lower their price by that same amount. In other words, the commission is always figured into the listing price.

MISCONCEPTION 3: BUYERS DON'T PAY BROKERAGE FEES; SELLERS DO, SO DON'T WORRY ABOUT IT

The problem with the myth that sellers pay the brokerage fee is that the fee is figured into the listing price. Indirectly, the buyer pays the fee. Absent that fee, the price would be adjusted accordingly.

Honesty is crucial in any interpersonal communication, especially in business. Unfortunately, leveraging lies continues to be one of the things real estate agents do best in order to stay in business. The following is a list of three of the most common things real estate agents lie about to secure listings, maintain viability, and cash in on a big commission.

1. **Representation:** Just because an agent works for a particular brokerage doesn't mean that all the listings at that brokerage are the agent's. Some agents may have website links to listings the prospective buyer believes belong to that agent, when they actually belong to other agents in the brokerage. This may not seem like a big deal, and in reality, it isn't. But how's that trust factor looking when that person has lied to you before even saying hello? If agents are willing to lie about listings, they're likely to lie about a lot more.

This is a good indicator that you should stay away from agents, and an even better indicator that you should negotiate the transaction yourself.

② **Experience:** Real estate agents are everywhere. Unfortunately, a lot of unskilled people see it as a get-rich-quick thing; they can get licensed very quickly and start earning big commissions right away. The reality is that a small percentage of agents close a very large percentage of the deals. Furthermore, experience is everything in this industry. Only experienced agents who have been through the grind several times and navigated through some tricky relationships for many years are worth anything at all. The experienced agents are still overpaid, but the inexperienced realtor has seen just about the same amount of wheeling and dealing as you have. If you're not dealing with a realtor who has at least fifteen years of experience, you definitely may as well do it on your own because chances are that you're just as capable of getting the deal done as most realtors are.

③ **Specialization:** "The Kondo King," "FHA Fanatic," or "Beverly Hills' Top Agent"—they're all hyperbolic brand names that mean absolutely nothing. Anybody can say anything is his or her specialty, but too many agents falsely announce such distinctions that have no real substance. They may bill themselves as a "Top Agent for Luxury Homes," when they've never closed a deal on any listing over $500,000. It's a particularly smarmy and unethical advertising gimmick because the only reason to hire an agent is for some sort of advanced knowledge or skill set that you *think* that individual has and you don't. So, if you know nothing about selling your condo and someone bills himself as "The Kondo King," the assumption is that person has knowledge you will benefit from. However, if that person has never actually sold a condo, that's blatant fraud, pure and simple.

Agents will try a whole host of other dishonest angles to try and justify their purpose in the real estate world. Some of them will even say they'll help you with something as painfully simple as your tax assessment or condo board package. That's as absurd as it is lazy, because these documents aren't that complex. In fact, they're not complex at all. In what world would you ever be willing to pay someone 5 percent of $400,000 to help you fill out a condo association package? That's like paying $1,000 for a pizza delivery.

HEAD GAMES

Going beyond mere leveraging of lies, most agents are very good at using psychology to take advantage of homeowners, particularly concerning the transaction side of things. They mask disconcerting head games as confidence in their own abilities with statements such as the following:

"You're going to need me to take care of all this for you. It's okay because it's what I do, and I don't mind holding your hand through all of it."

"This can be a very overwhelming process, so just bear with me."

"This is time-consuming, but don't worry because I'll handle everything."

"You definitely need a professional to stage this place and take good pictures."

"So much can go wrong with this transaction, but I'm here to take care of it all for you."

"Never fear, I'm going to get the two sides to come together, one way or another."

"This is going to get done because I'll see to it."

Whatever stage of the process you're in—whether it's pricing, exposure, or the actual transaction—real estate agents are always playing the same head game, which is that this is a difficult process, but they have the expertise to handle it. The reality is that the vast majority of them are very inexperienced and offer very little in the form of competence, but they're playing to your insecurities with this approach, and it usually works.

THE HOMEOWNER'S FEAR OF COMMITMENT

There's a public-scrutiny aspect that also comes along with putting up that "For Sale" sign in your front yard or even online. Once you announce that you're selling your house, you're committed whether you like it or not. There's no testing the waters, because you're officially committed to dealing with all the conversations about why your house is on the market. This is often a big deterrent to sellers.

For example, my mother is an investor who lives in a big house, and if it weren't for the public scrutiny involved in listing her home, she probably would have sold it by now. The problem is that she's not ready to jump in with a 100 percent commitment yet because she understands that the moment that house is officially for sale, she is going to get blitzed by an onslaught of agents. Her home is in a high-demand, low-supply zip code where there's simply not enough available properties to go around for all the potential buyers, so it's a realtor's dream come true. Unfortunately, she doesn't have an alternative way of testing the waters to look for qualified, legitimate buyers without slapping the "For Sale" sign on her home and incurring the bombardment of undesirables that comes along with it.

Most of this fear of commitment comes from a distrust of the middleman that we spoke of earlier. People naturally associate real estate agents with dishonesty and don't want to deal with them until they absolutely have to.

AMERICAN HORROR STORIES

Of course, not all real estate agents are bad people. The vast majority of them are socially responsible, morally sound, generally *nice* people. Although, even if Ghandi were a real estate agent, he'd still be virtually useless in today's online reality. The point is that I'm not highlighting the many *nice, but useless* real estate agents in the world. This section contains American horror stories about truly evil, bad-to-the-bone real estate agents.

Official Disclaimer: The following content contains graphic depictions of immoral, deceptive, and downright criminal behavior that has been attributed to the worst of the worst in the real estate agent world. It should not be read by anyone hoping to buy or sell a home through an agent, children under the age of thirteen, or anyone who wishes to maintain some sort of good faith and optimism in the greater good of humanity, the world, and life in general. *Reader discretion is advised.*

WHAT ESCROW MONEY?

We begin our macabre showcase of spectacularly unconscionable acts of misrepresentation in the real estate world with the story of former high-profile, Florida real estate agent Chris White. It seems Mr. White never met escrow money he didn't like—to use for his own personal expenses.

Back in January 2015 the *Sun Sentinel* published an article highlighting Mr. White's misdeeds, announcing he had been forced to surrender his real estate license and serve a three-year prison term for pleading guilty to defrauding clients of over $5.5 million.

It appears that Mr. White made it a part of his practice to pressure clients into handing him money to be put into escrow for the purchase of the high-dollar homes of their dreams. The problem was that he never put the money anywhere except in his own pockets.

Never fear, Florida home buyers, because not only is Mr. White resting not so comfortably in a Florida correctional facility, but evidently, his fraudulent activities weren't restricted exclusively to real estate. It seems Mr. White also misrepresented himself on his application for US citizenship. Therefore, upon release from prison, he will not be allowed to resume his fraudulent business practices, and instead, he will be deported to his native Jamaica.

SURE, I CAN HELP!

You know someone is running from something when that person operates under five different business names. That's a red flag that should never be ignored, and it's exactly what former Indianapolis real estate agent David Garden was doing while he defrauded his fourteen victims. Preying upon the desperation of many homeowners who were facing the foreclosure process, Garden stepped in and promised to help—or to help himself at least.

What he really did was scam these people under one of his many different business names, including Star Homes Inc., Garden Homes Realty, Christian Home Realty, and Five Star Realty. According to the *Indianapolis Business Journal* article of May 2016, he gained control of these properties with the declaration that he would help the owners with a short sale. Unfortunately for Mr. Garden, you can't put tenants in those properties and collect rent while you're busy *not* doing that. You especially can't do it if the property is in such deplorable condition that the court has issued vacate orders on it, which is exactly what he did in one case. In another case, he actually lived in the property himself, rent-free. Not a bad way to go if you can pull it off. To Mr. Garden's credit, he's still living rent-free—in prison.

BREAKING VERY BAD

What do you do if you find out the home you are trying to sell was once occupied by Walter White? Not exactly what happened to Dawn Turner, who now owns and operates the website MethLabHomes.com, but pretty close. According to an article in CREonline.com, Ms. Turner's son purchased a home in rural Tennessee, only to find out two years later, when he tried to sell it, that a previous occupant was put in jail for cooking meth at the home. Boy, did that deal blow up! (Ba-dum-bump, ching!) Fortunately for Mr. Turner, the blowup was figurative, and not literal. He did, however, have to pay an obscene total of $16,000 to have the site thoroughly decontaminated and deemed fit for resale once again. It seems that having a hazardous waste site loaded with deadly toxins is one of the few things that is not considered fair game in real estate.

I can just picture how the creative agent would position such a feature during a showing: "So...the kitchen has beautiful granite countertops, stainless appliances, and oh, by the way, the finished basement has a lovely wet bar, laundry hookups, and a meth lab if you decide to try a home-based business with high earnings potential."

Although many states have laws against this sort of thing, Tennessee, apparently, wasn't one of them. Buyer beware for home buyers in that state, I suppose.

THE AGENT'S FIREWALL

Out of the 110 million homes that presently exist in America, only about 2 percent of them are actively listed at any given time. A firewall exists within that vertical that is dominated by buyer's and owner's agents. If you want to sell your own home, and you think you'll use Zillow or one of those other websites, forget about it. None of the realtors trolling those websites are going to show your home without the promise of a commission of somewhere between 4 and 6 percent. You'll find yourself in the same position as our friend George Cahill.

THE SHADOW MARKET

The vast potential of real estate lies in the shadow market, which is the number of would-be sellers out there who want to sell their homes but don't want to deal with the biggest pain points such as public scrutiny, days on the market, and/or commitment to an agent.

By eliminating these pain points for the seller, and making the process simpler and more transparent for the buyer, emerging technologies can unlock the vast potential of the shadow market.

My company, EasyKnock, surveyed more than two thousand people recently, and 73 percent of the respondents said they would prefer an online portal to an agent. This survey included virtually every known demographic and socioeconomic background, all over the country. Additionally, 54 percent said they would sell their home if they could do it on their own terms. That's a very telling statistic because if there are 110 million homes in the United States, that means that 59.4 million homeowners would sell their home today if they could do it without an agent. This 59.4 million makes up the shadow market and illustrates the true power that new technology can bring to the consumer. It actually tells me two things: (1) people really don't like to deal with real estate agents, and (2) there would be a lot more homes for buyers to choose from if there were a better system in place.

Despite the preponderance of evidence that homeowners want to dispense with mediation in real estate, preferring to sell their property themselves, through technology, 91 percent of homeowners still use a realtor. Why is this the case? It's simple: there wasn't a reasonable alternative until technology emerged to force a change. The old FSBO route certainly wasn't going to get it done, but now peer-to-peer buying and selling has made real estate transactions infinitely easier to accomplish.

GIVE ME YOUR TIRED, YOUR POOR, YOUR HUDDLED MASSES OF FORMER HAND MODELS, SOAP ACTORS, AND PORN STARS...

Probably not exactly what Emma Lazarus had in mind when she first uttered a similar sentiment that would later be inscribed on the Statue of Liberty, but the header for this section suits our purpose quite well to explain how easy it is to be a middleman earning big commissions in the real estate world.

What does it take to be a real estate agent, capable of navigating the laborious legalese and pressure-packed negotiations in buying and selling everything from one-bedroom condos in East Los Angeles to palatial estates in the movie-star neighborhoods of Beverly Hills? In the state of California, until recently, not even a high school diploma. All you needed to do was pass the real estate exam, and you could sell George Clooney his next multimillion-dollar mansion. That's right, those of us not quite ambitious enough to go through all the trials and tribulations of taking a high-school equivalency test could, instead, opt for the real estate exam in California to try to earn a living...only in America, or at least California.

Believe it or not, most people don't graduate summa cum laude with a four-year degree in biomechanical engineering or nuclear physics to hock real estate. Realtors are usually individuals who find themselves landing there some years after school because their originally chosen profession didn't work out. Therefore, most agents are misfits. They're former auto mechanics, chefs, factory workers, teachers, nurses, even lawyers, and others.

Real estate agents come from all walks of life, but previous career heights appear to be no indicator of their ability to sell real estate. Even the best of the best in the industry can come from far less than auspicious backgrounds.

Consider the television show *Million Dollar Listing New York,* for example, which features some of the most wildly successful agents in the industry, who sell prime real estate in Manhattan, sometimes valued in the tens of millions of dollars, on a fairly routine basis. One of these agents is Ryan Serhant, a former hand model and daytime television actor. Not that there's anything wrong with either of those occupations, but the point is that he didn't exactly graduate from the Harvard Business School of Realty (which doesn't actually exist).

Another one of the show's stars is Fredrik Eklund. Fredrik used to be a porn star in Sweden. Not that there's anything wrong with that either, but he's not exactly a Rhodes scholar. Therefore, not to worry if that lifelong dream of being a rodeo clown doesn't work out, because there's always real estate. But that career crutch may soon be removed via recent superior technological advancements.

ONE HUNDRED YEARS OF THE MULTIPLE LISTING SERVICE (MLS)

The MLS was started as an agent cooperative in the late 1890s. Agents from all over the country would gather at local association offices to exchange information about their properties and agree to help each other sell their inventory. Its foundation was built upon one common goal: help me sell my inventory, and I'll help you sell yours.

Helpful cooperative or a foundation for a hundred-year tradition of collusion? Look at it whichever way you want to, but that's how it started. For agents, it ended up being extremely helpful, and it still is today. For consumers, it evolved into a necessary evil for many decades.

This business model evolved ever so slightly over the years, but it did not change all that much because the basic concept of MLS stayed the same for about a century. I'm sure in the very beginning there were some slight differences in the formalities of the meetings—such as, perhaps, the need for everyone to leave their shotguns on the table at the front desk, next to the tea and cakes—but not much more than that.

Until as recently as twenty years ago, all the listings of available homes would be shared in giant binders that were updated periodically in all the local real estate offices. Prospective buyers would stop by the nearest Century 21 branch and flip through the property listings with an agent.

Then, the advent of the Internet finally forced a major change to the way the MLS worked. Properties went online, and those giant binders full of available listings were probably thrown in a bonfire somewhere, most likely as part of some sort of ritual sacrifice to the god of exorbitant commissions and bright-yellow sports jackets.

WHAT AN AGENT CLAIMS TO DO

It was around the year 2000 when MLS officially went online. It produced an element of change in the way the system operated by allowing homeowners and buyers access to a virtual marketplace. Until then, agents claimed the following three vital objectives in the real estate world.

① **Transaction:** Here's a little-known industry secret: agents *never* do most of the work in a legal transaction. What they do is a great job of intimidating buyers and sellers into thinking they *need* them for this. In actual fact, it's the lawyers who handle the transaction process. After all, do you really want that California real estate agent who didn't pass the GED drafting up legal documents to put you in debt for $400,000? Don't want to use a lawyer either? No problem, plenty of online sites will provide you with all the real estate documentation you need to close a deal, all by yourself, for less than $100. It's really not that hard.

MISCONCEPTION 4: THE AGENT HOLDS YOUR HAND DURING THE TRANSACTION PROCESS

In reality, the lawyer does almost all of it.

---

② **Exposure:** This was the key realtor claim that online listings really eliminated. The Internet has replaced everything an agent could do in terms of exposure and made it better. Suddenly, with one click of a mouse, prospective buyers can see a comprehensive listing of the homes that are available in their price range. They don't even need to be at home to do this. Most real estate websites are mobile friendly and allow users to check out listings while riding the train home and passing through a dream neighborhood. No realtor in the world can match that level of exposure.

③ **Mediator:** The last bastion of hope that realtors are clinging to in order to avoid a dinosaur-like career extinction is that they claim to bring the two sides— buyer and seller—together. Due to trending AI technologies, we now have the ability to guide people to a price acceptable to both sides without any realtor's involvement.

WHAT AN AGENT REALLY DOES

What agents really do today is act as a severely overpriced tour concierge: they show properties. The first thing they do is put their mark on your property by placing their own brand of "For Sale" sign on the property and a lockbox on the front door. Once prospective buyers see your property online (completely irrespective of any realtor involvement), they usually call the listing agent, who meets them at your house, opens the lockbox, and gives them a guided tour of your lovely home. The agent shows them how many bathrooms it has, the upgraded kitchen, the big backyard for the kids and the dog to run around in, and whatever other amenities he or she can pitch about your property.

Are you really willing to part with 5 percent of a $400,000 sale for that level of concierge service?

In effect, that's what you're doing. Lawyers draft the purchase agreement, put money in escrow, and take care of the other necessary legal documentation. They make sure all the signatures are obtained and all the i's are dotted and t's are crossed. Meanwhile, an inspector comes in and gives it a seal of approval, and a title company does its thing too, but after the buyer sees your property and the two sides come to a price match, there's nothing else for the realtor to do. Is that worth $20,000? That kind of return could buy you anything from five thousand Skinny Vanilla Lattes at Starbucks to a brand-new, nicely equipped, convertible Fiat. It's obviously not an amount to be shrugged off as inconsequential.

MISCONCEPTION 5: THE AGENT'S COMMISSION OF 4 TO 6 PERCENT IS FAIR

Lawyers have always done the heavy lifting on the transaction side. The Internet takes care of the exposure side. And with emerging technologies, the mediation side isn't necessary either. All that's left for the agent to do is act as a tour concierge. Does $20,000 seem like a fair price for that service? The answer is: Of course not!

Until today, technology has focused on how to empower the agent even more, but I believe all that is about to change. The next generation of technology is going to go way beyond anything Zillow, Redfin, or Trulia has done. A good example of how these companies and their technology actually harms the consumer is in the civil war currently being waged within the real estate community between one of its elite agents, Ryan Serhant, and StreetEasy, a subsidiary company of Zillow.

IS IT "PAY TO PLAY" OR "BAIT AND SWITCH"? EITHER WAY, THE CONSUMER LOSES

In an article in *The Real Deal* of March 2017, Mr. Serhant blasted StreetEasy for a practice that I might describe as "pay to play," or even "bait and switch." Whichever way you want to look at it, the consumer loses, and to Mr. Serhant's credit, he recognizes that.

The practice Mr. Serhant blasted is EasyStreet's "premier agent" website feature, which lists the contact information for a premier agent—someone like Mr. Serhant—whom prospective buyers can speak to for more information on EasyStreet's website listings. The problem is that when consumers call the number listed, they don't get the premier agent's office. Instead, they reach an entirely different agent who paid StreetEasy to advertise on its platform.

Ryan referred to the process as "shocking" and probably "illegal." "Grossly unethical" may suffice to describe the practice, but Ryan also correctly pointed out that consumers really lose in this situation because they are being redirected to agents who know nothing about the listing. He also said, "There is no vetting process for agents who pay to get into the premier agent program other than providing a credit card number." In this scenario, consumers get an agent who is not only likely uninformed but who may also be completely incompetent.

This is a good example of technology gone wrong. Instead of further empowering mediocre agents who have done nothing but rest on industry laurels for the last one hundred or so years, what's needed is better technology to empower consumers.

CONSUMER EMPOWERMENT

The National Association of Realtors (NAR) is a trade association that protects the real estate community. It has a strong membership of more than one million professionals, which is somewhat scary because it proves how saturated the industry really is. The NAR was founded in 1908, so it's been advocating for the real estate professional for more than one hundred years now, which begs the question of who has been advocating for the consumer during all those years.

Until now, nobody has been protecting the buyer or seller in the real estate industry. I'm hoping to change that in a couple of ways. One is with my company, EasyKnock, and the other is by forming the Consumer Empowerment Residential Re-Tech Organization (CERRO). The mission of that organization will be to empower consumers with emerging technologies and cutting-edge programs to help them get a fair deal in any real estate transaction.

Chapter 2

REAL ESTATE 2.0

———

The new era has already begun. Four alternative versions of buying and selling real estate have been available for more than a few years now. The following four methodologies provide good examples of the new direction real estate is moving in.

① **Discount Agents:** This is a lot like buying a Vizio instead of a Sony or Samsung television. Discount agents will charge as little as 2 percent to help you sell your home.

There's an inherent flaw in the discount-agent business model, however. Companies can't involve a broker and be too discounted in the current real estate environment, because the overhead will drive them into bankruptcy. That's exactly what happened a few years ago to a discount firm called Foxtons.

Foxtons entered the New York City market with a discount-agent model that scared the sports coats off the rest of the agents in the area because Foxtons started charging commissions as low as 2 percent. When that didn't work, they raised it to 3 percent, and then 4 percent, until it just didn't work at all, and they filed for Chapter 11 bankruptcy.

Discount agents may seem a good idea, at first glance, but there are a few problems that prevent discount services from being a long-standing solution.

Ⓐ You may have to do a lot of the leg work of marketing and showing your home on your own, which begs the question of why you don't just sell it yourself.

Ⓑ Some buyer's agents may be reluctant to present your property to their clients if they know they will receive a discount on the commission.

Ⓒ A high-priced, low-value agent is still involved in the process, creating too much cost and thus rendering the business model unworkable.

Discount agents aren't much of a technological advance, but at least they provide a step in the right direction of a more reasonable commission.

② **Flat-Fee Agents:** Although still a little on the unusual side, flat-fee agents are a nuance of the real estate world that is just starting to gain a little popularity. These agents will agree to sell your home for a fixed price, no matter what the sale price of the home is. It doesn't matter if you have a one-bedroom condo with a shared bathroom or a $10 million luxury estate with twelve bathrooms, still a flat-fee agent charges you the same amount. The favorite response from traditional realtors to this market niche is, "You get what you pay for." I don't necessarily agree with that opinion, because I don't think traditional realtors should get a bigger paycheck just for selling a bigger house. Whether it's the one-bedroom condo or the luxury estate, most of the work involved is identical, so why shouldn't agents take a flat fee, regardless of the listing price? For that reason, flat-fee agents aren't a bad option, but you're still paying someone to perform very little service.

③ **À La Carte Services:** This business model has found its way into a lot of industries recently. Cable television providers are finally starting to offer à la carte channel selection, so you don't have to subscribe to fifteen different versions of the Home Shopping Network if you don't want to. À la carte real estate—although still fairly uncommon—allows the seller to pick from a menu of real estate services. For example, you can pay $50 for each showing of your home. Or maybe you just want to pay $30 for a photographer to take pictures of your home. Another menu item may be to have your house professionally staged for $75. These prices are all entirely fictional, but I quote them here just to drive the point home of what an à la carte offering might look like.

④ **Resellers:** Nationwide networks of real estate investors such as HomeVestors of America (aka "We Buy Ugly Houses") will give you cash quickly for your home with little to zero closing costs. The benefit to using one of these services is that you get money in your account faster than any other way of selling your home. It's especially useful if you're in a personal bind, such as divorce, job loss, or emergency. They'll also buy your home "as is," so there's no need to go through a massive renovation just to get your house ready to sell. The problem with these services is that you'll sell your home at a somewhat significant discount, usually anywhere from 6 to 10 percent of market value.

FSBO

The preceding list of four alternatives to traditional real estate serves as more of a bridge to a newer FSBO methodology fueled by technological advances than as a permanent solution. These alternatives may provide some value beyond the traditional way of doing business, but they don't facilitate a true peer-to-peer buying and selling process.

A symbiotic relationship between peer-to-peer transparency and technology will be at the heart of the new era of real estate. We're not talking about your grandfather's FSBO here. For many reasons, what was known as FSBO thirty years ago just didn't work the way it should. The future of the FSBO market, however, will be rooted in technology rather than solely on people's sheer determination to eliminate the middleman.

There's a public misconception that the FSBO market is a huge one these days. Sadly, just the opposite is true. It peaked around 1985 when it represented a full 25 percent of the marketplace. The latest figures have it at barely over 7 percent.

In 2017 sites such as Zillow and ForSaleByOwner.com serve mostly as lead generators for agents to solicit you. EasyKnock recently performed an experiment with a small sampling of individual sellers. We had these people list their homes as FSBO. Out of the number of calls the sellers received, what do you think the percentage of agents to potential buyers was?

Sixty percent in favor of agents?

Nope.

Seventy percent?

Wrong again.

Ninety percent?

Still not right: Ninety-seven percent of the calls were from agents trying to secure the listing.

THE FSBO REVOLUTION OF 1985: WHY DID IT FAIL?

What likely happened in the years around 1985 was the first real attempt at a revolution in real estate. Homeowners finally found a way out of giving away 6 percent of the sale of their home to opportunistic agents. Savvy sellers around the country began putting up FSBO signs on their front lawns at unprecedented levels. The biggest problem was that the only way potential buyers could contact you for a negotiation was if they happened to drive by your house, and at forty-five miles per hour, someone else in the car (hopefully not the driver) just happened to see your sign and either was able to memorize the phone number or was lucky enough to have a paper and pen in the car to write it down. You can see where the logistics just don't add up to success here.

Another problem with the FSBO revolution of 1985 was that homeowners severely underestimated the survival instincts of the real estate agent. The industry began using the FSBO sellers' own tactics against them by flooding their phone lines with calls offering to *help them* sell their home. Morning, noon, and night FSBO sellers would answer the phone in hopes of a potential buyer wanting to see their home, only to hear, on the other end, something such as. "Hello, is this Mr. Cahill? My Name is Buddy Kane (the toothy real estate guru from the movie *American Beauty*). Did you know that I guarantee I can help you sell your home in less than two weeks?" In this scenario, not only would Mr. Cahill hear from Buddy another two or three times before the end of the month, but he would also hear from countless other Buddy Kane types. Therefore, battered and bruised, the FSBO real estate revolution of 1985 ended up as a failed coup. As a result, the old guard stood triumphant and remained in power for the next few decades.

Yet another problem with the current FSBO market is that agents know they're not going to get a "pocket listing" out of it. A pocket listing is when an agent works both sides of the transaction—acting as the agent of the buyer and the seller, which is so unethical—yet, somehow, legal—that it's scary. And the agent keeps the entire commission. It's hard for an agent to pocket-list if one of the parties is trying to skip paying commission. FSBO works against buyers because their agent is unlikely to be proactive in the FSBO market. In other words, finding a home for their buyer in the FSBO market would work against the agents' competing agenda of trying to secure a pocket listing.

MISCONCEPTION 6: REAL ESTATE AGENTS WANT TO FIND YOU THE BEST HOUSE FOR YOUR PERSONAL WANTS AND NEEDS

Actually, they'd exchange anything for a two-sided commission, regardless of how well the house suits you and your family. Most of them would sell a one-bedroom condo to the Duggars if they could and it meant a pocket listing.

The drop in FSBO activity is a serious anomaly in the ongoing trend of today's overall business environment. Technology has served as a catalyst for a DIY mentality in almost every other industry in the world, except real estate. However, homeowners are just now starting to pick up on the variety of technological tools that are at their disposal to buy and sell homes by themselves. Look for FSBO activity to increase dramatically in the next three to five years.

THE INCREASING DO-IT-YOURSELF (DIY) MENTALITY OF TODAY

Earlier, we mentioned how most of the millennial generation would rather work with a computer than a human. It could be trust, simplicity, or even comfort, but it's causing some interesting parallel trends as well. Coinciding with that preference for technology is the expansion of the do-it-yourself (DIY) mentality of millennials.

Understanding that labor accounts for approximately half the cost of any home-improvement project, the younger generations are implementing a DIY strategy to get ahead in life. Due to the skyrocketing price of homes and our must-have society, every opportunity to gain a monetary advantage is golden. For most do-it-yourselfers, it goes beyond financial benefits. They enjoy the creative aspects and the satisfaction of a job well done.

Technology is contributing more every day to the DIY phenomenon. For instance, it seems instructional YouTube videos are available on everything from installing high-quality hardwood floors to performing open-heart surgery and safely landing on the moon.

Most millennials would rather do their own research, book their own vacation, and even grow their own food if they could. It makes sense that those growing up in this generation, or beyond, would also prefer to buy or sell their own homes. The theory of disintermediation of real estate is consistent with the DIY trend of younger generations because it's flat-out a better process, and younger people, who are most comfortable with technology, can see that, perhaps even a little more easily than the rest of us.

THE ONGOING DIY TREND IN REAL ESTATE

DIY real estate, as it currently stands, is going to require an investment of your time, and in today's society that's a big investment. You'll have twelve-hour work days, commuter traffic, kids to feed, soccer practice, sporadic social events, visiting family, cleaning the house, walking the dog, and—if you're lucky—ten free minutes to yourself per week to drink wine or watch something on Netflix—*if* you're lucky.

So, although technology is rapidly changing and DIY real estate is soon going to require less time than ever before, the first thing you need to do is accept this commitment of time. Some of those things we just listed are going to have to wait. Hire a dog walker, pay someone to clean the house, and give the kids a granola bar every three hours, between meals, if you have to. In the end, a little extra effort on your part is going to pay huge dividends in finances and getting the home you really want. Besides, the time you must commit to buying a home on your own isn't that much more anyway.

Even with an agent, you still have to show up to take a look at multiple homes before you find the one that fits your lifestyle and your vision of a dream home.

You still have to be there to sign at closing, which will be signing as you've never signed before. By the end of this process, no matter which writing method you choose, you could incur some form of carpal tunnel syndrome from signing your name over and over again for well over an hour.

You still need to talk to a mortgage company, or multiple mortgage companies, to get the best terms for your particular wants and needs.

When considering all these factors, your DIY time commitment is pretty much the same as it would be if you were to engage a high-priced agent, so you may as well do it yourself. The potential bonus in doing something yourself lies in not having to work with anyone you trust less than yourself.

IT'S A MATTER OF TRUST

The National Association of Realtors estimates that as much as 50 percent of all FSBO listings are sold to someone the seller knows: a friend, a friend of a friend, a relative, or perhaps a colleague who just happens to know about the listing through word of mouth, which is a form of trust. The seller obviously trusts this person because she knows him and can personally verify his viability as a buyer. It's a good example of how trust can be an integral part of a good business relationship.

Another good example of how trust can work in business is when you choose Angie's List over Craigslist. The people on Angie's List are vetted through their online reputation and consumer reviews, so trust is key in transactions on that site. Sellers on Craigslist are...well, they're on Craigslist, and most of us know who and what's out there on that site, which doesn't add up to a whole lot of trust.

The same sort of evaluation process that Angie's List offers is also offered by other successful websites and apps such as Airbnb and Uber. They all provide the consumer with a system for assessing the other party's validity. Therefore, what's needed is for technology to work the same way in residential real estate. Does it seem that far-fetched that an online real estate marketplace could be created that rates and reviews all the participants based on some commonsense variables? It shouldn't, because the technology is obviously already out there and being put to good use in other industries.

Beyond mere ratings and reviews, a well-designed trust system for new online real estate websites should offer features such as prequalification letters, credit ratings, LinkedIn profiles, licenses, and so on. By using these different qualifiers of trustworthiness, consumers will become increasingly comfortable with using such a system, and this form of verification will be key to the new FSBO real estate model that has already begun to evolve.

HOW WILL IT WORK?

The new real estate FSBO revolution will feature a dramatic shift in the way properties are bought and sold. Not only will the users be properly vetted through a trust system built into the website design, but what we earlier referred to as the shadow market will be unveiled, meaning more than fifty million previously *unavailable* homes may attract bidding and, ultimately, be bought and sold. We may see a serious influx of residential real estate activity once the trend achieves widespread acknowledgment and usage.

One element of new real estate websites will be a database of existing properties, whether for sale or not, where people can look up what homeowners might be willing to sell their houses for without being committed to actually selling them. It will be similar to something you currently see on Zillow, except it will include an indication of the price at which the homeowner would be willing to sell.

The site will offer a page with prepopulated information on a number of key variables—home style, number of beds and baths, square footage, and so on. Homeowners can input what price they would be willing to sell their home for.

For example, your house could be worth $500,000, but you might state that you're only willing to sell at $575,000. At that point, the engine would allow potential buyers to log in with their own verified and secure user credentials and bid on the house. If you get a lot of bidders, you're probably priced too low. If you don't get enough bidders, you might be priced too high. It's an element of unprecedented price discovery, far superior to merely pulling three or four neighborhood comparisons.

The price-discovery process will be very simple, but logical, and it won't require a commitment from anyone for anything until a match is made and an agreement is settled. There is a limit, however, to this period of noncommittal because some accountability is necessary at some point. You won't be held responsible until you agree to make a match with the prospective buyer. Once that match is made, you can still pivot away from the deal if you want to, but your rating will be lowered, as your credit rating would be if your car were to be repossessed. That hit in your rating may be enough to make it difficult to use the site anymore, but that's a good thing because it's a sensible way of ensuring the legitimacy of the site and all its users.

Additionally, evaluation tools will be set up to provide an estimate of what experts think your home is worth. These tools won't be your standard, run-of-the-mill evaluation tools you see on so many other sites today. They will take into account advanced metrics that factor in trends, history, and more to get a much more accurate evaluation than what's passed as acceptable at this point within the industry. You can decide if you want to factor that estimate into your desired price point, or if you want to ignore it completely, go rogue, and set your own price. The choice will be yours.

If you're thinking, "Well, I can get evaluations on Zillow already," don't forget Zillow's revenues come from the real estate agent industry, so Zillow's numbers don't necessarily reflect what's good for the average homeowner, nor are they even very accurate. In fact, a recent article in the *Washington Post* reported that Zillow's estimates only get within 5 percent of the actual value of a home 41 percent of the time. That's a big margin for error on well over half of the market, which means Zillow's estimates are not very accurate at all.

The article goes on to say that the best way to find out what your property is really worth is *not* by using Zillow or by talking to an agent. It's by putting your home on the market to see what people are willing to pay for it. An even better way would be to find out what people would pay for it without having to commit to putting it on the market. It's a worry-free, commitment-free, modern-era form of price discovery that's been long overdue in the real estate industry.

EMERGING TECHNOLOGIES AND PLATFORMS

The new technologies that foster peer-to-peer relationships, a fully vetted online verification system, and an opening of the shadow market will provide several other smaller but welcomed benefits to homeowners and buyers alike. Consider the following highlights that are sure to follow.

- The public scrutiny of listing your home will be removed because you'll be able to test the waters without committing 100 percent to the sale of your home and announcing to the world that you're selling it. It's an improved version of price discovery.

- Price discovery will be quick and easy because all customers will have access to the tools, resources, and information they need to negotiate and close the deal themselves.

- Dishonesty and distrust of realtors with a competing agenda will no longer exist, because there will be no need for a middleman to muddle transparency.

- Homeowners will save the 4 to 6 percent commission they would otherwise have to pay to a realtor.

- Buyers will save 4 to 6 percent off the price of the home because homeowners won't have to build it into the price.

- Buyers and sellers will be able to open and close the entire transaction process, empowering consumers everywhere to sell on their own terms.

- Access to lawyers, title companies, inspectors, and everyone else needed to get the transaction completed will be provided if necessary.

- One simple user interface will be used that will guide customers step-by-step through the entire process with little to zero confusion and definitely no realtor jargon or double-talk.

A few companies are already implementing some new features that are having a positive impact on the industry. Although none of them yet go the distance in completely eliminating the middleman the way my company, Easy-Knock, will (see the appendix for more information), at least they serve as proof of the existing trend away from the traditional way real estate has been bought and sold for over the last one hundred years. Consider doing some additional research on the following companies to get a feel for what is on the rise in residential real estate and the global marketplace.

First, the resellers:

Opendoor: Opendoor buys homes from sellers at a discount. Then, the company markets those homes to prospective buyers from its website. The company puts a keypad with a lockbox on the door of the property, and buyers can go check it out at their leisure with no influence from realtors. It's an interesting niche because when we spoke about millennials earlier, we talked about their preference for technology over personal interaction. It provides a nice alternative for any prospective buyer who falls into that category. Furthermore, they've implemented a highly usable interface in their online process, making it even more attractive to tech-savvy buyers. You will, however, be selling at a discounted price.

OfferPad: Request an offer, and you should get one from them within twenty-one hours. This company doesn't use advanced technology as much as it tries to eliminate the pain from the process. They want to make things happen fast and hassle-free for their clients. It seems to be an option that best serves people who want to get out of their homes fast. There could be anything from an ongoing divorce to pending litigation or even a meth lab (ahem) that sparks such a motivation. One way or another, if you need to get out quickly, OfferPad might be the way to go. The caveat is the same, however, as it is for the other resellers: you will be getting out fast, but you will be doing it with less profit.

Knock: Not to be confused with my company, EasyKnock, this is an interesting twist on the reseller subgenre. It's an online platform that guarantees sellers their home will be sold within six weeks or the company itself will buy it at market price. They do a nice job of integrating technology by allowing you to use their interface to talk about your home and get an offer quickly. They also have a mobile app, just in case you want to sell your house while you're bored at the opera one night.

Although Knock has a nice thing going with its sales guarantee, it still involves using an agent, which—discounted or not—still comes with a litany of pain points for the buyer and seller.

All these resellers take some of the pain out of selling by giving you quick cash up front, but they do it at a substantial discount from market value, which still ends up costing the seller money. What's really needed is a platform that takes the technology these companies employ and combines it with a full-scale, peer-to-peer buying and selling process with no discounts and no competing agendas.

Now, consider some other companies that are influencing the way real estate is evolving in different ways:

Compass: This company has earned a valuation of more than a billion dollars. It is, essentially, trying to carve out a niche in the industry by specializing in certain markets.

Currently, it offers services in New York City, Miami, Greater Boston, Aspen, Los Angeles, Orange County, Washington, DC, The Hamptons, Santa Barbara, Montecito, and the San Francisco Bay area. Their claim is to offer elite agents with unsurpassed service and resources. However, a recent article by *The Real Deal*, a popular online real estate magazine, reports the following: "Critics from within the industry say it's just a brokerage firm masquerading as a technology company, while admirers see it as the brokerage firm of the future."

Compass boasts state-of-the-art technology with some of the best talent in the industry, but who cares about the talent? If the technology is good enough, buyers and sellers should be able to do it themselves with no interference, no competing agenda, and most importantly—no commission.

Ten-X.com: Formerly known as Auction.com, and in agreement with my own thinking, this company says it is "one more reason real estate is moving online, and the old ways are going, going, gone."

Billing itself as America's leading online real estate marketplace, Ten-X allows users to buy and sell properties completely online. According to the website, the company does what it does "by combining millions of anonymous Google search queries with our own up-to-the-minute transactional data to create the industry's first model that isn't just accurate; it's weeks ahead of traditional indicators."

Ten-X uses advanced analytics and technology to offer commercial, foreclosed, and move-in-ready properties through three different subsidiaries: Ten-X Commercial, Auction.com, and Ten-X Homes. Although their commercial and foreclosed listings have been around for some time now, the Ten-X Homes website, which offers move-in-ready homes and more traditional services, has only been online since March 2016.

Purple Bricks: A British online real estate platform, Purple Bricks is, essentially, a flat-fee broker that offers two different methods for selling your property: you can choose either to sell your property through an assigned and dedicated local property expert or to sell by auction. Either way, you're given access to highly usable technology, including an app that gives you instant feedback from showings, and you're given full support throughout the process.

Purple Bricks certainly seems like a good example of combining technology with excellent service to create a better process. However, the service still lacks true disintermediation.

Reali: (Pronounced "really?" Maybe not, but it just comes out that way whenever I say it.) Whichever way you say the name, this company is essentially an online dating website for buyers and sellers. You don't meet for coffee and exchange phone numbers or anything like that, but the company makes matches of buyers and sellers through mobile technology. The app also features bidding and a live expert chat feature.

Faira: It seems that Faira is attempting to bridge the gap between technology and human interaction. The site attempts to automate whatever it can in the real estate process but uses actual humans whenever the situation calls for it. Is it enough disintermediation to help, or is it a mere nuance or gimmick that only further complicates an already complicated situation?

Blockchain: This company is a model of disintermediation of the very financial system we have all come to know and sort of love. By using technology inspired by Bitcoin, Blockchain wants to empower consumers everywhere to have more control over their finances by implementing a digital currency to replace traditional cash dollars and cents. Think of the U.S. Department of the Treasury as the real estate agent whose time has come and gone in this scenario.

The idea of Blockchain is creating significant buzz among technology leaders, economists, and even conspiracy theorists everywhere. By using a cryptocurrency such as Bitcoin, this technology has the power all on its own to change the real estate industry in more ways than one.

Remember our friend Mr. Chris White from the section on American horror stories? His crime was based on his deceitful, dishonest, and disreputable nature. He was a high-profile agent who took people's money and exploited their trust. Instead of putting their money in escrow where it belonged, he pocketed it for his own use. Using Bitcoin has a distinct advantage in this scenario, because there's no paper currency, personal check, or bank account transaction to pocket. Blockchain is software, and with it, you can program an escrow amount. Therefore, people like Mr. White simply won't have access to those funds, because they will be electronically programmed to be available for one person only—the bank, or whoever else is supposed to receive them with his or her own electronic key or password verification. Without proper electronic access privileges, people like Mr. White will need to make their living honestly instead of criminally.

Blockchain has the further ability to eliminate fraud completely from real estate by using digital ownership certificates, which would make false ownership virtually obsolete because these certificates are just about impossible to replicate. It's much easier to print counterfeit money than it is to duplicate cryptocurrency. By the same token (pardon the pun), it's much easier to make a fake identification, title, or other paper proof of ownership than it is to make a fake digital certificate.

This concept goes one step further, virtually eliminating the need for not only agents but notaries, inspectors, escrow companies, title companies, and government property databases as well. Consider the following quotation from the November 2, 2015, blog of Jason Ray, a technology executive and operations leader:

> Blockchain will enable every property, everywhere, to have a corresponding digital address that contains occupancy, finance, legal, building performance, and physical attributes that conveys perpetually and maintains all historical transactions. Additionally, the data will be immediately available online and correlatable across all properties. The speed to transact will be shortened from days/weeks/months to minutes or seconds.

If Mr. Ray's prediction of Blockchain's capability comes true, the world of real estate will never be the same. There will be no more waiting sixty days to close on a house; it might be done in sixty seconds. Better book the movers now, I guess.

If the idea and popularity of Blockchain doesn't tell you that technology is changing the real estate industry, then perhaps nothing will. It's one very big way in which technology is making a better process by eliminating pain points and removing the middleman from the equation entirely. It's an example of streamlining a system to its maximum efficiency and ensuring more secure transactions at the same time.

THE STRONG WILL SURVIVE

For the honest, hardworking real estate agents who are performing well in today's market, there will still be ample opportunity for sustained success in the new marketplace. There's room in any industry for the people who fit this profile.

Eventually, machine learning will likely take over a lot of industries—as much as 47 percent within the next decade or so, according to a recent infographic published by Futurism.com. However, for the next ten to fifteen years in real estate, there's going to be an interim period when the true professionals in the industry will merely be repurposed and serve different roles.

Real estate professionals who endure the evolution of their business will reap the rewards throughout this interim period in two ways.

1. Disenchanted agents and those who are merely going through the motions will be driven out by the challenges presented by the new marketplace. This will cause a survival-of-the fittest trend in which only the best of the best in the profession are left standing. A weeding out of the mediocrity in the industry will benefit the survivors because they will be the only game left in town.

2. Better technology will lead to process efficiencies, which will also translate to higher volume for the much fewer remaining agents.

Once again, I'm harkening back to my days in the personal-equity sales business with institutional sales people. That industry went from rooms full of fifty or more brokers to just two or three. However, volume exploded for those elite brokers who were left. They went from executing seven or eight trades per day to five hundred. Certainly, commissions per transaction were drastically reduced, but the sheer volume more than made up for it.

Emerging technology should do the same thing for the elite real estate agents that it did for the elite institutional sales rep from twenty years ago, but they're going to have to tough it out while the industry evolves.

PART 2

DISINTERMEDIATION IN OTHER INDUSTRIES

Chapter 3

THE MELTING ICE CUBE

———

Thomas Friedman's new book is called *The Age of Acceleration*. In it, he describes 2007 as the most pivotal year in history, largely due to the birth of such technologically advanced devices as the iPhone. All of a sudden, people had the power of the Internet, access to e-mail, and even the ability to play Angry Birds right in their pockets at all times. Previously, flip phones and other similar devices tried to include some form of Web browser, but it was a hopelessly laborious task to do any sort of real Web-browsing on them.

It was the iPhone that put the whole world in our hands. That was the start of having nearly limitless information at our fingertips at all times. For the previous twelve or so years of popular Internet usage, people had to retreat to a desktop or maybe a high-powered laptop to get answers to their questions. With the iPhone, people suddenly had the ability to get answers while at work, on the train, walking to get lunch, or on the couch while watching *Mike Tyson Mysteries*. The World Wide Web became a virtual and portable version of the *Encyclopedia Britannica* and much more.

Soon after, Facebook began its foray into the social fabric of our lives, and the world was never the same again. Other social-media sites had existed before that. The original one that is now defunct was Six Degrees, and then Myspace took over for a while. But it was Facebook that brought the world of social media into the lives of virtually every man, woman, and child over the age of thirteen. What does this have to do with the iPhone, you ask?

The combination of the two wildly successfully inventions spurred an era of engagement with the typical consumer worldwide.

But that was just the beginning.

In his book, Friedman goes on to talk a lot about Moore's Law, which describes an observation that was once made by Intel cofounder Gordon Moore in 1965. He noticed that the number of transistors per square inch on integrated circuits had doubled every year since their invention. Based on that observation, Mr. Moore predicted that sort of exponential technological growth was likely to continue for the foreseeable future—and it has.

The era of expanded consumer engagement took off with the iPhone and Facebook back in 2007, but its growth went positively ballistic from there. Moore's Law held very true in regards to how these technologies—the Internet, smartphones, and social media—have worked in conjunction with each other to form unprecedented growth in consumer engagement and peer-to-peer communication around the world ever since.

TRENDING DISINTERMEDIATION THROUGH TECHNOLOGY

What happened after 2007 was a trend toward disintermediation that was fueled by the rapid growth of readily available technology. Suddenly, people started communicating through their smartphones with more than just a simple phone call. Texting gained instant popularity. People were checking in on Facebook and tweeting on Twitter. Even the least tech-savvy consumers began to learn a whole new method of communication through a device that had just been invented, and from it, a whole new way to buy and sell products and services arrived as well.

Despite humble beginnings as an online book retailer, Amazon allowed people to buy great products online without having to go to a brick-and-mortar store and talk to a sales associate. Goods would arrive in two business days or less with no shipping costs, and customer service provided quick and easy returns when necessary. Sites such as eBay took consumer engagement to new heights, allowing people to sell their old baseball cards, used video games, and everything else they had stored in boxes in their garage over the last twenty years.

When people can connect with each other directly without the interference of a middleman, they can get to the bottom line and clearly understand each other much more easily. It's also a more efficient and much more cost-effective way to buy and sell. Middlemen are time-consuming and expensive, and they muddle transparency. Consider the following examples of hugely successful companies that have completely removed the middleman from their business model:

The biggest retail company in the world is Amazon, but it owns almost no retail space and employs zero salespeople.

The biggest document company in the world is Docusign, but it doesn't employ a single in-house lawyer.

The biggest cab company in the world is Uber, but it doesn't own a single cab or employ a single cab driver.

It's easy to see that not only is the trend of business eliminating the middleman, but the companies that have successfully executed that strategy have become the biggest operators in their respective industries.

Drawing upon my experience on Wall Street, I remember the old days when investors who wanted to buy a stock would call their agent. If the orders were large, investors would call an institutional sales desk and the salesperson there would try to find a seller. For their time and services, the salespeople involved would take fairly large commissions. Fast-forward to the way things are done today, and it doesn't matter if investors want to buy 100 shares or 100,000 shares; they don't need to call a broker anymore. They can do it by themselves with a standard laptop and a high-speed Internet connection.

That level of disintermediation on Wall Street cut commissions by 90 percent over the last fifteen years, which is an astounding number, enough to make Donnie Azoff (Jonah Hill's character in *The Wolf of Wall Street*) go on a cocaine bender long enough to make his brain spontaneously combust into a million fractured pieces of greedy, gray gunk.

Consider how some other companies have pioneered various aspects of consumer empowerment through advanced technology:

Uber pioneered premium logistics with its user-friendly app and supreme accessibility.

Amazon pioneered levels of service that were previously deemed impossible with its massive global warehouse strategy and way-ahead-of-the-curve use of robotics.

Airbnb pioneered the trust factor. Prior to Airbnb, people were very reluctant to let someone into their homes for fear of—well, getting murdered, among other things. Since Airbnb came into existence, people are not only willing to open their homes to complete strangers, but they'll also do it for complete strangers from faraway countries they know nothing about.

THE NATURE OF CAPITALISM: SOMETHING BETTER ALWAYS COMES ALONG

All those industries—taxis, retail, and hotels—already had good processes in place, but no matter how good a process is, something better always comes along. All products and services have a life cycle, even if the process appears to be operating at maximum efficiency. Eventually, technology will enable an improvement—either in speed, complexity, or quality. One way or another, something better always comes along.

Consider the following examples of how other once widely accepted processes have been changed by technological innovation:

Knowing how to hail a cab was a rite of passage for every New Yorker worth his salt. But ride sharing was just a flat-out better process. Instead of standing on the roadside curb with your hand in the air, as you get splashed with a pungent burst of mud puddles and city sewerage every so often, you can now order a ride from the comfy confines of your home through your smartphone while making a cappuccino to go. Which one would you rather do?

Ordering from the Sears catalog to have merchandise arrive at your door was a good-enough process back in 1985. Sure, it took a few weeks to show up, and you probably had to pay for shipping, but it was fine, until Amazon came along and made it much better. Now you can get your order in two business days and *not* pay for shipping.

Staying in a hotel, motel, or bed and breakfast was also a good experience—usually. However, Airbnb not only lets you stay in a home with many more amenities than most short-term living accommodations but also allows you to operate your own home like a hotel, while you're gone. It's another good process that was made even better. Going on vacation? Why not rent out your home while you're away to help pay for your own stay? This is what we call a clear-cut win-win.

Think disintermediation is limited to ride sharing and long weekends in London? Think again. Today's trend in disintermediation features a rise of the robots through advances in AI that's happening everywhere. However, be on the lookout for the T-800, Model 101 (The Terminator)—you've been warned!

WHERE'S THE ROBO-BEEF?

There's even a company called Momentum Machines, which provides automated gourmet hamburgers from scratch. Previously, the idea of processed food had people thinking Twinkies, Ring Dings, and other spongy pseudofood with enough artificial preservatives to survive a nuclear holocaust. Now, automation is geared up to produce not only fresh food but sophisticated culinary creations for the discerning palette as well. Momentum Machines also does it at a reduced cost.

Momentum Machines has the backing of tech experts and top restaurateurs from the San Francisco Bay area (an area that knows a thing or two about great food). Their process starts with freshly ground beef, which is grilled to order by a robo-machine, which then tops the burger with a variety of condiments and fresh produce. A gourmet bun finishes off the burger, and it's all done with a minimal investment in the machine by the restaurateur. After the initial recipe and system is perfected, the restaurant never has to hire a cook again, maybe just a machine operator for regularly scheduled maintenance.

HERE COMES THE ROBO-WOLF

No, I'm not talking about some sort of robotic lycan from the next horrible incarnation of the *Underworld* movie franchise. I'm talking about the use of robo-advisors for investment firms. Financial institutions with a rich history and a solid reputation such as Charles Schwab, Fidelity, and others are using automated investment advisors. These money-making machines use different variables such as historical data and your capital allocation needs to serve as private wealth advisors. The companies that are using them claim that robo-advisors can manage wealth more efficiently and at a significant discount compared to the more traditional broker-based client relationships.

What's next, self-driving cars? Oh, wait a second...

INSURING DISINTERMEDIATION

Ordering home or apartment insurance by calling an insurance agent wasn't the worst thing in the world— or was it? It took about twenty minutes on the phone to describe how close you were to the fire department, if you were in a flood zone (believe me when I say pray to God that you're not, because it can get *very* expensive if you are), and if you had a trampoline on your property, just in case that seemed like a good idea for some strange reason. It was a somewhat time-consuming, personal interaction that you didn't need to add to your already overcrowded to-do list for the day. Nonetheless, it was better than physically going to the insurance agent's office to do any of it.

Progressive started the revolt against the insurance agents by offering quotes from multiple companies online in about five minutes. All you had to do was put up with their weird commercials featuring that pasty-skinned and somewhat overly vivacious spokesperson, Flo. Now, companies such as New York City-based Lemonade are offering instant everything. Lemonade offers quotes, claims, and everything else that insurance agents can do through an app on your phone, featuring the distant relative of Siri, Lemonade's insurance bot, Maya. Why deal with an agent or even Flo for insurance when you can just install Maya on your smartphone, and have her at your beck and call to indemnify you before someone careens off your trampoline and suffers a severe head wound?

HEY, TAXI!...NEVER MIND, I'LL JUST CALL FOR AN UBER INSTEAD

How can you tell when you've taken an industry's business model away and made it better? That's easy: they sue you! That's why the New York City Taxi and Limousine Commission are in a seemingly perpetual court battle with Uber. Ride sharing has provided such an improvement in better service, a friendlier interface, and cheaper fares that taxi drivers have just about nowhere else to turn. So, off to the courts they go in a last-ditch effort to stave off complete elimination.

You can't fight capitalism, as long as it's legal.

The pace of technology is accelerating, and the ice cube of the old world—pre-Internet and pre-consumer empowerment—is melting. Better ways of doing things are being developed all the time. The real estate industry has fought this battle hard and staved off elimination for longer than most industries, but the time has simply come for a better process for buying and selling homes. In fact, it's overdue. The process of doing business with a real estate agent was effective enough for a long time, but it's become one filled with dishonesty, red tape, and a lot of lost dollars. Fortunately, for buyers and sellers of today, a new process is rising, and it's up to you to take advantage of it.

Chapter 4

ESTABLISHING A BETTER PROCESS BY ELIMINATING PAIN POINTS

———

Now that we understand how disintermediation has affected those industries by creating better processes, let's investigate what it is about those newer processes that make them better than their predecessors. Start by reflecting on the following industry-specific questions:

Why is ordering an Uber better than hailing a cab?

Why is point-and-click shopping on Amazon better than going to Sears or Kmart?

Why is handling all your insurance business on your smartphone better than calling a local agent?

The biggest reason all those processes are better than the old way of doing business is the elimination of the pain points inherent in those older processes. I don't have any idea who originally uttered the words, "No pain, no gain," but the deceased comic legend George Carlin had a much better take on that quotation: "My philosophy is... no pain, no pain."

Hailing a cab in New York City on a cold and windy night in October has never been fun. In fact, it's downright miserable, potentially dangerous, and painful.

Going to Sears and dealing with some sad sack of a 1950s-style salesperson in a tweed sports coat to buy a vacuum cleaner—although somewhat amusing—has never been fun.

And calling an insurance agent to spend twenty minutes on the phone talking about the lovely new home you just bought, only to get a quote at the end of the conversation that doesn't meet your needs, expectations, or budget—forcing you to call another agent and start the process all over again—is also very painful.

The newcomers in all those new industries took away those pain points.

By the same token, selling your home through a real estate agent with a competing agenda is sharp-stick-in-the-eye painful. Therefore, the number-one goal of the new way to buy and sell real estate through far more efficient technology and sensible disintermediation is to eliminate a seller's pain points, which are as follows.

① Public scrutiny

② Days on the market

③ Commitment to an agent

④ Paying an unreasonably high commission

The next four sections discuss each of these pain points in detail and how the new way to conduct real estate will eliminate them.

PUBLIC SCRUTINY—LIKE IT OR NOT, YOU'RE ALL-IN

The "For Sale" sign goes up on your front lawn, and immediately your nosey neighbor, Mrs. Gladys Kravitz (of 1960s pop-culture fame from the television show *Bewitched*) starts the buzz around the neighborhood about why you're selling—divorce, job loss, witchcraft, or anything else Mrs. Kravitz can come up with—and the rumors abound. It's an aspect of public scrutiny that immediately puts you in the spotlight, and not a pleasant one, either. It's an all-in process. There's no such thing as testing the waters in the traditional real estate model. You're either selling or you're not.

If you're in the FSBO market, you're all-in. The process involves constantly answering phone calls from agents who ask why you're selling your house and who tell you how they can *help*. Unfortunately, this sort of help really is a four-letter word because true help doesn't usually involve a 5 percent commission amounting to the loss of tens of thousands of dollars.

The new real estate model will promote the idea of never having to be all-in. Your house will always be listed on the new real estate websites, and the choice will be yours as to whether or not you want to entertain offers. People will never see your house as "officially for sale," but if you're an active user, you could, all of a sudden, one day just accept an offer to sell your house because..."They made me an offer I couldn't refuse." (Yes, I just went from quoting the hokey 1960s sitcom *Bewitched* to paraphrasing what's widely considered to be one of the greatest films of all time, *The Godfather.*)

By eliminating the pain point from the public scrutiny that comes along with being all-in, the new real estate model will open up communication among consumers, increase transparency, and put money back in consumers' pockets rather than the pockets of an agent who did very little to earn it. Think of the new real estate model as testing the waters rather than being all-in.

DAYS ON THE MARKET—LIKE IT OR NOT, YOU'RE ON THE CLOCK

Another thing that happens as soon as you declare to the free world that your house is officially "For Sale" is that the clock starts running. One of the more highly visible negotiating factors in a real estate transaction is the number of days on the market. The general principle behind "days on the market" is that the greater the number, the weaker your negotiating position as a seller is, especially if you're on the market for more than ninety days. Then, people start thinking about what could be wrong with the property—flaws that aren't immediately apparent. They start questioning their own sense of good judgment. In a nutshell, you raise suspicion, which is never good for business.

The pain point for the seller here is, once again, concerned with an all-in approach. If you're just testing the waters rather than being all-in, then the days-on-the-market variable is no longer applicable. It's a nonfactor, and that evens the negotiating process for the seller to get a fair and equitable deal.

MISCONCEPTION 7: YOU NEED TO SELL YOUR HOME AS QUICKLY AS POSSIBLE

This is not necessarily true. Although a variable such as days on the market can be seen as a negative by buyers in the traditional real estate model, home-owners should be able to test the waters and do an extensive amount of price discovery before committing to anything and starting the clock that creates this false belief in the need to sell right away.

COMMITMENT TO THE AGENT—TRUSTWORTHY OR NOT, IT'S STILL PAINFUL

There are two relationship scenarios that can play out when you're fully committed to dealing with an agent to sell your home, as follows.

① **Dealing with an agent you trust and like:** In many ways, this is the worst of all agent relationship scenarios. The agent could be a friend, a family member, or someone else you trust and genuinely like. If that's the case, then along with that relationship comes pressure and guilt. You know this person is working for commission. Therefore, you feel this tremendous pressure to get the deal done, so she can make some money to feed the kids, make a mortgage payment, or even buy a dream car—everybody and every situation is different. In this scenario, you're much more likely to accept a subpar offer that meets your agent friend's agenda, but not necessarily yours, because you want to see this person get paid, and you definitely don't want to feel as if you're withholding something from your agent friend.

② **Dealing with an agent you don't completely trust or necessarily like very much:** Sometimes, this is the easier scenario to deal with because you can usually just tell this person to hit the road if you feel he is not performing due diligence for you. However, if you're not particularly strong-willed, then it's easy to feel pressure from a less scrupulous real estate professional and get coerced into doing something that you did not want to do.

Either of these two scenarios is a big pain point for the seller. The pain comes from the stress of guilt and pressure.

By using my concept of a newer, technologically based real estate model, you automatically rid yourself of this pain point because you're dealing more with technology than salesmanship. In fact, the salesmanship becomes obsolete because you're inputting your terms into the website engine and dealing directly with the other party with no intermediary to muck it up.

MISCONCEPTION 8: AN INHERENT TRUST, DUE TO A SHARED DESIRE TO GET YOUR PROPERTY SOLD FOR AS MUCH MONEY AS POSSIBLE, IS BUILT INTO THE RELATIONSHIP BETWEEN THE HOMEOWNER AND THE REAL ESTATE AGENT

Unfortunately, this isn't true, because the number-one complaint about most agents is dishonesty. They don't care very much if your property sells for its premium market value. They just want to get the deal done fast. This creates a competing agenda, which has the byproduct of distrust.

COMMISSION—WHATEVER IT IS, IT'S TOO MUCH

Typical real estate commissions in the United States run somewhere between 4 and 6 percent. By the way, America has one of the highest commission-based pay scales for real estate agents in the world. Actually, France for some reason can even be a little higher, but most countries fall somewhere around 3 percent. In Great Britain, most agents are paid just 1.5 percent and, instead, earn a yearly salary to make up the difference. The strange thing is that most British real estate professionals prefer the salary with lower commission because there's more guaranteed money. Regardless of international commission rates, let's work with three numbers to see what an average US agent's commission could mean to you if you can put that money in your own pocket instead:

TABLE 1

LISTING PRICE	AGENT COMMISSION BASED ON 5 PERCENT	WHAT IT MEANS
$250,000	$12,500	A luxury vacation for the whole family
$500,000	$25,000	A nicely equipped new car that could last ten years or more
$2,500,000	$125,000	A college education at most good state universities

When attempting to soak these figures in, understand that the average lawyer's paycheck for this transaction is probably going to come to somewhere between $2,000 and $3,500. Also, realize that it's the lawyer who's protecting you and doing almost all the dirty work in this transaction. She's the one drafting the legal documentation that keeps everyone safe and makes sure the deal gets done without any carny tricks or unethical shenanigans. By that standard, it's the lawyer whose price should go up exponentially according to sale price because the lawyer's services are what are protecting your assets in the transaction. Therefore, does it make sense to anyone who isn't an agent that agents, who do little more than present the home and make a phone call when an offer is made, should reap the reward of such a lopsided increase based on the mere listing price of a home?

If it all seems so unfair that agents, who may have little more than a high school education, as opposed to lawyers, who had to withstand law school and pass the bar exam, make so much more money on real estate transactions, then how did this system get so dysfunctional?

Central and positively crucial to the idea of disintermediation in the real estate market will be the fact that percentage-based commissions will be gone. There's so simply no reason for anything but a flat fee in the process of buying and selling a home. That flat fee may increase or decrease based on the amount of work involved, but it will usually be around 1 to 1.5 percent, which sure isn't anything close to the drastic disproportion you see in Table 1.

The process just evolved that way. Collusion by agents back in the late nineteenth century created a system that prevented people from selling their own homes, or finding a better way to do business.

The buyers just wanted to know what properties were available at the time, and the realtors were happy to present more properties by working together. As time wore on, however, Internet-based technology made access to the available properties frighteningly easy, and lawyers took over the transaction side. However, the old way of doing business continued because a better process simply never presented itself...until now.

We said before that technology drives change, and we're in the midst of an unprecedented period of technological breakthrough right now. Technology is changing the way everything is done, and real estate should be no different.

Moore's Law is still firmly in effect, and now AI is providing us with advanced analytics that were never possible before. Also, the DIY nature of Internet-savvy users in the younger generations is making previously unavailable options on the Internet available, and users all over the world are able to do more online than ever before. We just need to seize the opportunity of a better system as it presents itself and make it work for the betterment of everyone with real estate to buy or sell in the future, as well as now.

Chapter 5

ARTIFICIAL INTELLIGENCE: FORGING THE NEW PATH THROUGH IMPROVED ANALYTICS

———

Many websites such as Trulia allow you to do a search based on a few basic variables to find homes available for purchase in your area. You can give the system a price range, number of bedrooms, and style of home (condo, detached, etc.), but that's about it. That's not the kind of AI I'm referring to in my new technology-driven real estate model. In fact, that sort of collection of metrics is the C- student in this picture. The AI I'm referring to in emerging technologies will allow for a much more robust search, enabling superior results with an unprecedented level of precision based on your input.

Newer technologies such as HouseCanary are offering products that feature much more advanced metrics. There are a lot of things about a home that make it more or less valuable besides just the number of bedrooms it has and whether it's a condo or single-family dwelling. Today's AI can accommodate requirements such as a mountain view and a near-water location. It's capable of factoring in historical data, economic trends, and other nonphysical key determinants of property values and forecasts.

SETTING THE BAR FOR ADVANCED ANALYTICS

HouseCanary: Most recently, an analytics company called HouseCanary raised $33 million. The company provides "on-demand access to the industry's most accurate home valuations, forecasts, and market analytics." It offers comparisons, an estimate evaluation tool, and an appraisal tool. The company is not competing for origin but is highlighting the reality that the industry is evolving very quickly with much more precise analytics driven by superior technology.

Quantarium: You know a company is brashly confident and cutting-edge when it describes its technologies as "disruptive." Quantarium, based in Seattle, Washington, employs some of the best engineering talent available to provide highly advanced real estate analytics that are dynamically adaptive to new data sources.

According to its website, the company targets its services at "astute customers who engage innovative approaches." In other words, they seem to be a perfect fit with the new way to buy and sell real estate.

SELLING WITH ADVANCED ANALYTICS

Understanding that price discovery should be based on much more than a mere listing of neighborhood comparisons—which is just about the only thing an agent will do—this shining beacon of big data at work uses the following factors in its valuation process and more.

- Macroeconomic data

- Data from capital markets

- Mortgage records

- Search and social data

- House and parcel data

- Assessor records

- Pricing trends

- Property attributes as compared to other local homes

- Home-improvement history

- Local market inventory

- And yes, MLS listing information and local sales data

Through complex algorithms that take all these factors into consideration, HouseCanary boasts a nationwide Median Absolute Percentage Error (MdAPE) of 5 percent, as of February 2017. These complex algorithms are also weighted based on regional nuance, which could include everything from weather conditions to unemployment rates. They also run thousands of simulations for each property they track. It's a big data warehouse for real estate buyers, sellers, and investors alike. HouseCanary has all the analytics needed to make great real estate decisions with zero input from an agent.

Comparatively, an agent will show up at your home and bring a listing of four to five comparable sales prices in your neighborhood, which you could find out on your own via Google or maybe two to three telephone calls. That, however, will be the extent of the market research an agent will do to determine a sales price for your home. With this in mind, it's easy to see how technology is surpassing the subpar, archaic skill set of that profession.

MISCONCEPTION 9: WITHOUT AN AGENT, PEOPLE CAN NEVER REALLY KNOW WHAT THEIR HOUSE IS WORTH

The reality is that modern technology with advanced analytics enables price discovery far better than anything an agent can provide merely with local comparisons.

BUYING WITH ADVANCED ANALYTICS

By using more precise technology, buyers and sellers should be able to make more precise decisions. Technology will be able to take certain demographic information about each user and find suitable properties, not solely based on the basic variables they input for what they're seeking in a home, but also based on personal characteristics. In other words, if I let the engine know that I'm fifty-five years old, Orthodox Jewish, and participate heavily in temple activities in New York, the system should be able to take all that into consideration when finding a suitable property. Therefore, the system should also be able to bring up homes that are within walking distance of a temple and suitable for someone over the age of fifty-five.

The same degree of accuracy should be available for the user profile of a twenty-four-year-old who has a lot of similarly aged friends, follows Captain Morgan's on Facebook, and frequently uses taxi services. In this case, the system should bring up properties in neighborhoods with a plethora of bars and coffee shops, and maybe a shopping mall. Single-level condos are probably a safe bet as well. Either way, the AI should factor in variables such as proximity to a temple or bars, socializing or stay-at-home types, and youthful versus older-adult communities.

AI APPLICATIONS ALREADY IN WIDE USE

Better analytics have already forged a new path in many industries. Need proof? Think about how you perform a Google search for something, such as a new car. If you Google a 2017 Cadillac SRX just to see its general specifications, fuel mileage, and cost, what do you think is going to happen the next time you're on a website that sells advertising space? It's going to show you an ad for the 2017 Cadillac SRX. Need more proof of how advanced AI is working its way into the way we do things? Consider the following three examples that exemplify it best:

1. **Netflix:** This is a company to be admired in many ways. Netflix began as a rental service for DVD movies through the mail in exchange for a monthly subscription fee. That was its original business model, which proved to be a relatively short-lived one because streaming and downloading content on-demand became so popular so quickly that Netflix had to adjust. And adjust it did. In fact, it not only began its own streaming service but also began developing its own content, because it recognized the way the industry was evolving. Netflix's corporate survival instincts showed it needed to evolve, and that's what it did.

   With a little vision and a lot of understanding of how technology affects every marketplace, Netflix successfully evolved from an online version of Blockbuster Video to an actual content provider. Therefore, it makes good business sense to understand that Netflix may just have good forecasting abilities through excellent analytics.

   A big way in which Netflix passes the benefits of advanced analytics to the consumer is through its recommendations system on its website. Every time you log in, you're likely to get a customized listing of movies and television shows that Netflix is recommending you check out based on your previous viewings. In fact, this list of recommendations is so good that it factors in who is watching when you log in too. After logging in to your account, you need to tell the site who is watching before you can go any further. What's most significant about this subtle nuance to Netflix's user interface is that it's usually a very accurate reflection of movies you really do want to watch. For instance, the site is not going to recommend the redux of *The Texas Chainsaw Massacre* if you tell the site that your four-year-old daughter is looking for a movie to watch.

② **Amazon:** When Jeff Bezos—or Amazon, as a company—speaks, it's a good idea to listen. Amazon has successfully built the largest warehouse distribution system in the world through great vision and tireless dedication to providing superior customer service.

A more detailed look at Amazon's success reveals that the company is astoundingly good at using big data to make its business run like a well-oiled machine. It uses advanced analytics in a lot of ways. In fact, there's a popular story going around that Amazon's data are so good that the company preemptively moves products to different centers before purchase because Amazon knows when people are most likely to consider purchasing that product. The company also points out items you've recently viewed whenever you're logged in to your account, and it makes suggestions—similar to Netflix—for other products you might want, based on your purchase history. In other words, if you search for Star Wars Snuggies on Amazon, you're likely to get a cornucopia of Star Wars products offered to you the next time you log in to your account—T-shirts, underwear, posters, coffee mugs, probably even jewelry. Of course, you will also likely see a wide selection of Snuggies. But let's face it. You deserve everything you get with that search.

③ **LinkedIn:** This is advanced analytics for professional networking in action. LinkedIn has positioned itself as a must-have in the professional world. If you're not on LinkedIn, chances are that professional networking just doesn't matter to you. The website provides a constant flow of people you may want to connect with, based on whatever similarities LinkedIn's analytics indicate are relevant. The purpose is to network among like-minded professionals. It's sort of the new-age version of picking up the "Help Wanted" sign at the local downtown print shop circa 1957. LinkedIn provides this notification system on its website and in e-mail messages to you on a fairly frequent basis. It does things such as notify you of potential job matches, personal connections, and the opportunity to endorse someone's skill set. For instance, you can endorse your coworker's superior underwater yodeling skill if you happened to witness it in action at last year's company Christmas party. Actually, you can endorse it even if you didn't witness it. Unfortunately, there's not a whole lot of vetting going on with this process, but LinkedIn is changing all the time, so who knows what the future has in store?

Technology is leading the way to disintermediation in real estate. Many other industries have already experienced the phenomenon, and the consumers in those areas have reaped its many benefits. The final few chapters will tell you how you can benefit from the middleman's elimination in real estate, and how easy it will be to participate.

PART 3

DISINTERMEDIATION IN REAL ESTATE AND HOW YOU CAN BE A PART OF IT

Chapter 6

THE FUTURE IS NOW, AND IT'S MUCH EASIER THAN YOU THINK

———

Contrary to what real estate agents want you to think, buying a home is *not* rocket science, and the disintermediation of real estate is merely the result of a trend in recent consumer behavior. We live in a world virtually controlled by technology, arduously monitored by social media, and justly rewarded by an independent, DIY attitude. The trends of the younger generations are showing a preference for technology over human interaction and DIY over delegation. Here's what the process of buying (MS in rocket science notwithstanding) and selling a home should look like.

FIVE STEPS TO BUYING REAL ESTATE WITHOUT AN AGENT

The mortgage process is really separate from the home-buying process. We're assuming that everyone knows the first thing you need to do is get preapproval for a mortgage. If you're not aware of this, it's crucial to understand that the preapproval amount will likely be in the neighborhood of seventeen million times more than what you can actually afford. The moral of the story is that it's up to you to make sure you calculate your budget carefully and determine what you can afford for a mortgage, irrespective from what that preapproval states.

An agent does just about nothing in the mortgage process, either, unless you want to go with the agent's recommended "guy" to get a mortgage, which I don't recommend, because that will be feeding into the agent's collusion. Plenty of banks and credit unions are extremely willing to give most consumers a mortgage. In fact, it's how they make money, so they want to work with you, as long as you're a good risk.

Before enacting these five steps, get your preapproval letter, and the bank will work with you on getting the mortgage when the time is right during your process. All you have to do is keep the bank in the loop while you go through the following five simple steps to buying your home in my vision of a real estate world without middlemen.

① **Do the research:** By going online to perform some simple research, I don't mean you should go on Realtor.com and start searching for houses. What I mean is you should first get some specifics on what's important to you.

Find out which neighborhoods have a low crime rate if that's important to you (and it probably should be).

Is your dream neighborhood close to not only your own and your spouse's or partner's jobs but also close to industry in general, just in case you move on from your current roles, as people do so often these days?

Find out if there's public transportation nearby, if that's a factor.

Look up what the schools are like if you have kids.

Advances in AI have made investigating these variables much easier recently. There are already plenty of great websites at your disposal that will allow you to learn all about these things. For example, GreatSchools.org is a free service that will give you an excellent rating system to determine whether or not a favorite neighborhood of yours has an acceptable school system. It's worth noting that it's obvious this website takes into account more than the simple letter grades of graduating students. It's another good example of advanced analytics in action.

Over the next five years or so, advanced AI will take your research abilities way beyond just verifying if a school system is acceptable or not. Soon, you'll be able to run very specific searches to find the perfect house. You'll be able to tell the system if you're sixty-five years old with COPD and need to be near public transit, or if you're twenty-five years old and not only need to be within walking distance of seventeen different local bars, but those bars also have to have at least fifty different beers on tap and make killer chili nachos.

② **Find your home:** You can use the plethora of online real estate search engines to find your dream home. Newer technologies are going to incorporate a more comprehensive search with better algorithms, but there are plenty of ways to skin this cat. Go online, and find three or four desirable choices to further investigate as possibilities for your dream home.

There are a lot of homes out there, and don't forget, with new technologies such as EasyKnock entering the picture, you won't be limited to just 2 percent of the homes in America. Your search will be opened up to the previously untapped 98 percent of the market, which amounts to around 110 million homes that currently exist in the United States. Take your time, and search comprehensively. Also, it helps to realize that there's always going to be a better home at some point. Just when you think you've moved in to your forever home because you love it so much, another one with even bigger bedrooms and a nicer kitchen will surface, eventually. The moral of this story is not to hedge too much over making your selection of a dream home, because other possibilities are always just around the corner. Buyer's remorse is a fairly normal emotion during the home buying process, but try not to get too caught up in it, because a better home will always come up and there's nothing you can do about that.

MISCONCEPTION 10: THE MARKET IS LIMITED TO THE 2 PERCENT OF HOMES THAT ARE LISTED AS AVAILABLE

Realistically, there are millions of homes that would be sold if the homeowners could directly connect with potential buyers and sell on their own terms.

③ **Schedule a showing:** Time to go kick the tires on a few houses. A lockbox should be provided at whichever home you want to see. A lot of agents no longer bother to appear at the showings anyway. So, this part of the process might not even be that much different.

Don't get too caught up in microlevel thinking here. You're going to hire a home inspector later in the process anyway, one who isn't tied to the collusion and competing agenda of an agent. So, he's very likely to give you an honest assessment of the condition of all the home's valuable and expensive parts. Let him take care of examining the foundation, checking for termites, and other minutiae that could be costly if ignored. Your job is to take a look at each of your final contestants and see if you like the flow, number of bathrooms, size of the bedrooms, layout of the kitchen, and other more obvious and easier-to-judge items.

④ **Make an offer and negotiate:** How often do you think a first offer on a home is accepted? That's right, almost never. Understand that part of the normal buying process is to make an offer somewhere lower than what you're expecting to get the house for. Then, the seller will counter, and as long as you're both bargaining in good faith, a deal should get done relatively soon. That's right, a deal should get done. Realtors don't have some sort of magic deal wand they secretly wave in the air to hypnotize both parties until they come to an agreement. It just takes a certain amount of commonsense and reasonableness on each side, and the deal gets done regardless of what the real estate agent says or does.

Be prepared that if you lowball with your initial offer, the homeowner may be insulted and not counter at all, or choose to break off negotiations with you, permanently. It's also good advice not to fall in love too quickly or too hard with your dream home, because this part of the process can be a lot like a used-car negotiation.

When trying to buy a new or used car, all you can do is make a reasonable offer and be prepared to walk away if the salesman just won't bargain in good faith. It's been part of the consumer's dance with the car dealer for decades now. You should take the same approach when looking at a home. If you make a reasonable offer, and the homeowner doesn't reciprocate in good faith with a reasonable counter, then you should be prepared to walk away as you would if you were dealing with Sal's New-to-You used car lot and trying to buy that 2012 Mercedes convertible with low mileage.

(5) **Get some hired help:** The first form of professional assistance you're going to want to acquire is a good lawyer. After the negotiating process has been fulfilled and an offer accepted, it's time to contact a skilled attorney, one who knows all about real estate law. This is when agents tell you how hard they're working to get the deal finalized. In reality, they've simply handed over the brunt of the paperwork and legalities to a law school graduate, who is actually capable of handling such a transaction. Meanwhile, the agents are driving off in their Lexus, trying to convince another buyer to do the same thing.

The official documentation and legal portion of the process varies state-by-state, so it's crucial that you have an attorney working for you who is in the same state, or at least familiar with your state's real estate laws. You'll see samples of standard real estate contracts all over the Internet. Don't pay too much attention to any of them, because there is no such thing as a one-size-fits-all real estate contract. Every deal is different. These online samples are just templates that need many items added and/or taken away, depending on each individual transaction. While they may serve as a fair-enough general guide, they should not be considered as a perfect reference point.

Next up on the hired-help list is to get a good inspector. My vision of a technology-based real estate platform will give you access to fully vetted and trustworthy inspectors. These professionals will have no ties to a real estate agent in your situation, so they will itemize every aspect of the home that may need attention, investment, or work. This list will make up the contingencies of the sale. At this point, you will negotiate those contingencies with the seller. This is one of those situations in which the agent is likely to tell you how hard she is working for you. Bulls**t! It's easy enough. You just decide who will pay for what. For instance, if there's a serious issue with the roof, then, maybe, you decide to split the cost. Once again, as long as both parties are negotiating together in good faith, the deal will get done. You don't need a real estate agent to give you the he-said-she-said after every phone call with the other party. If anything, this sort of mediation makes the process more complex and is more likely to get one or both parties all riled up. After that's out of the way, you may want to split the list of smaller items so that neither party bears the full expense of getting the home in perfect condition.

Lastly, ensuring a clear title is another process that agents have nothing to do with but make it look as if they do. Just as with the inspector and the lawyer, there's no need to conduct this search on your own, either. The newer technologies will incorporate finding these professionals in a simple-to-use interface that provides ratings and a full vetting system.

After you've hired all the help you need, it will be time to close. Your lender, lawyer, inspector, and title company should hold your hand through the whole process, right up until closing time. This is when you just show up—usually at the title company's location—and sign about 175 different pieces of paper.

That's it! You're done buying a house, and you didn't have to deal with a middleman and her competing agenda throughout the process. Oh, and chances are you also saved somewhere around $20,000. Does that seem worth it? You bet it does!

This is a generalized system for what things look like without a realtor's involvement. Specific technologies will have their own brand and interface for buyers to use, but the system should look something like the preceding five steps. For a more detailed view of the EasyKnock process of buying and selling real estate, take a look at the appendix in the back of the book.

THREE STEPS TO SELLING REAL
ESTATE WITHOUT AN AGENT

(1) **Do the research:** Whereas buyers research a variety of neighborhoods for potential matches with their requirements, sellers need to research their own neighborhood. As a seller, you should start by going online to find three to four houses in your area that are considered comparable to your own. That will provide you with the comparisons, which is just about the most exhausting task a real estate agent will do for you. Once that's done, you can do some real price discovery.

You can use a website such as HouseCanary to find a more accurate estimate of what your home should sell for. Now it's entirely up to you to decide if you want to use this valuation, or maybe, you're not 100 percent convinced that you want to sell right away. Maybe, you'd like to test the waters by listing a price that is $10,000, $20,000, or even $30,000 higher than what seems to be an accurate market value. That's okay too. The real beauty of the new real estate model is you don't have an agent breathing down your neck the whole time to lower the price. You decide how willing you are to negotiate and how badly you want to sell. There's no all-in commitment in the new technology-driven real estate model.

② **Set the stage:** It's time to make your house as pretty as possible and to take some pictures. As we learned earlier, when we discussed à la carte real estate services, you can hire people to stage your home, take pictures, and show it if you want. Or you can save even more money by doing it yourself because it's not that hard. After all, most of us do have those smartphone things on us at all times that just happen to take good-enough pictures.

Before touching the snap-picture button on your phone, however, you need to stage your house appropriately. This isn't hard, either. Eliminate clutter, move some furniture around if necessary, and take some good pictures of the best features of your house. Don't be misleading in any way, but take pictures of your home that show it in its best light. In other words, there's no need to take pictures of the fenced-in area where the dog goes to do his business. But if you have a jetted tub as part of a spectacular master bath with heated tile and double vanity, then by all means, you should snap a picture of that.

Don't think taking great pictures is all that important? Think again, because they can actually be a deciding factor in how many showings you get and, ultimately, how many reasonable bids you receive.

In fact, pictures may play a bigger role in our society today than ever before.

We live in a country of braggarts. Pinterest and Instagram are loaded with people taking pictures of a steak dinner they had the previous night. They want to boast about the dry-rubbed, Angus, bone-in ribeye, along with the mashed cauliflower and blue cheese and pear salad they "experienced" at Chez Overpriced Steak House. And don't forget to look at the overpriced $100 bottle of wine on the side.

Social media is also loaded with selfies of wannabe models posing in the full-length mirror, while blowing a kiss and wearing microscopic lingerie to show off their midriff, five weeks after childbirth.

People attending live theater post photos on their Facebook timeline just to show the world, or at least their close circle of friends, how cultured and sophisticated they are, or at least want to be known as.

It's a trend that's consistent with our capitalistic society, and that's good for business because it works in your favor. New real estate platforms will encourage people to take pictures of their beautiful homes—even if they're not for sale, and they just want to show off. As a homeowner, it's not a bad idea either, because those show-off pictures may be just how you get someone to fall in love with the remodeled kitchen, decked-out man cave, or lavish landscaping. This could easily be the way you receive an offer that comes close to that $10,000-over-market-value asking price you listed.

③ **Lawyer Up:** After showing your house to a few prospective buyers, if someone places a bid and you negotiate an agreeable set of terms, then you'll want to hire a lawyer to take care of all the dirty work for you.

For the seller, that's really the end of the process. Can you believe that people are still willing to forego $25,000 of the sale price on a $500,000 home? It's really all about finding the right buyer. Once that's done, the deal almost takes care of itself, and whatever is left over gets handled by the lawyers from both sides. Technology has simply surpassed the skill set of real estate agents, and soon, the consumer will be empowered to put that technology to good use and save tens of thousands of dollars in the process. It really is that easy, and it's happening now!

Chapter 7

PARTING ADVICE

———

Who knows what's going to happen to the economy. Nothing is set in stone.

Unemployment rates rise and fall with the wind.

Social Security is not a locked-in source of income for anybody expecting to retire ten years from now.

Even retirement plans such as 401(k)s that were seen as the failsafe for a secure retirement have suffered vicious ups and downs.

One thing that remains the same, however, is that your home continues to be your biggest asset. It's the very reason you leave that one-bedroom apartment near all the great coffee shops and restaurants you like to frequent.

You paid rent in that place for years and received no equity in return. With a home, every time you make a mortgage payment, you're gaining equity. Therefore, it's easy to see how crucial effective handling of that asset really is. With that in mind, you think you need to hire a professional to help you buy or sell it. The problem is what's become of that industry over the years.

The legacy of real estate agents has morphed from helpful professionals with a limited, but semivaluable skill set, to professionals with a competing agenda that generates distrust, dishonesty, and collusion and severely diminishes their worth. In fact, their value in today's online marketplace, among an entire population of tech-savvy users, is marginal at best.

How hard is it to look up properties online?

How hard is it to look up lawyers online?

How hard is it to look up inspectors online?

How hard is it to look up title companies online?

You get the picture...

Is it worth $25,000 to you for a realtor to schedule show-ings of your $500,000 home, and make phone calls when an offer is submitted? It sure doesn't seem it. Hopefully, by reading this book you now have the awareness, the knowledge, and the confidence to buy and sell property completely on your own. Companies such as Opendoor, HouseCanary, and EasyKnock are changing the way real estate sales are transacted.

Opendoor is creating a frictionless process for people to sell their homes quickly at a discount.

HouseCanary is providing better comparisons with increasingly advanced analytics.

EasyKnock is allowing sellers to test the waters without any of the pain points involved with an agent. It's also opening up the marketplace to prospective buyers of the other 98 percent of homes in the country that aren't listed as being available on the market.

Disintermediation in real estate is not a hard concept. Remember that most of the brokers these days just print off comparisons from sites you use anyway. Readily avail-able technology already allows you to see homes you like, schedule tours, negotiate, and hire a lawyer—all without the pain, aggravation, and tens of thousands of dollars for a real estate agent. The new process is well worth the small amount of time you need to invest to take advantage of it. *You can do this!*

Appendix

THE EASYKNOCK WAY

Companies such as Opendoor and OfferPad have already implemented an alternative to buying and selling residential properties in the traditional manner, which involves a middleman. Therefore, the future is definitely now. The revolution has already begun, and you *can* be a part of it. My company, EasyKnock, aims to be a leader in that revolution, a forerunner of how the new process will take shape, eliminate pain points, and empower consumers.

Formerly, if you were interested in buying a house, you would physically knock on the door. EasyKnock opens up that door to everyone's house online with zero public scrutiny, no worry about the number of days on the market, and absolutely no commitment to the agent. For more information, go to www.EasyKnock.com. You can also

just read the following quick summary of our process to
see how it will work:

THE NEW TIER BETWEEN FSBO
AND ACTIVE SELLER

① **Claim your profile:** A prepopulated profile with
basic statistics including the year a house was built,
the square footage, and other basic data for every
homeowner in America who wants to be found will
be available. The first thing interested homeowners
do is claim their profile.

② **Enhance or edit your profile:** No system is perfect.
If the system mistakenly lists three bedrooms, but
since it was last updated, you added a bedroom, then
you can make that change to your profile. You'll also
be able to add pictures, videos, and perhaps some
other nuances that make your home more appealing to
prospective buyers. Whatever changes you make will
cause the system to revise the valuation of your home
in real time. This is where the vetting system comes
into play. If you state that your home has a lovely
master suite with jetted tub, walk-in shower, double
vanity, and heated tile, when in reality, what you have
is a handmade, wooden outhouse with a magazine
rack stocked with 1970s issues of *Playboy*, then you're

going to get some negative feedback from prospective buyers, which will be appropriately reflected in your rating. The legitimacy of a true peer-to-peer relationship is crucial to the effectiveness of our system, and we will be doing everything to safeguard that.

③ **Answer some questions:** We have two questions: (1) What would compel you to sell your home, and at what price? (2) On a scale of one to five, with one being "just testing the waters" and five being "ready to sell," how motivated are you to sell your home? It's as simple as it sounds; answer these two questions, and move on.

④ **Become vetted:** There's a very short vetting process involved, just to weed out the various undesirables and jokesters of the world. I know. Who would use the Internet just to blow off some steam, play a prank, or wreak some havoc, eh? Oh yeah, lots of people. That's why we will likely ask for something such as a picture of your driver's license or some other form of verification to, once again, maintain the integrity of the system.

⑤ **Check for bids:** After homeowners claim their profile, answer those two questions, and become vetted—in all, a process that should take around fifteen minutes—they will be able to see if anyone is interested in bidding on their home, who is bidding, and at what price.

(6) **Chat with a chosen bidder:** Homeowners now have the ability to select one of those bidders at whatever price they announced, and start a chat with them. Keep in mind that the bidders are also vetted. Therefore, any bogus bidding or fraudulent activity of any kind will be reflected in their ratings as well. We advise treading carefully in this process because it can work a lot like a credit score, where one repossession or foreclosure can just about ruin your credit for years. Similarly, one dishonest representation or outright lie could shatter your rating on the website and loudly announce to other users that you are not a good candidate to do business with. Buyers will likely be vetted with such documentation as a mortgage prequalification letter, a FICO score, a LinkedIn profile, or other superior-quality forms of identification and credit worthiness.

The chat between seller and buyer should center on when to schedule a home viewing. You can be home for this viewing, but the logistics of it are entirely up to you and the buyer. The only difference between a showing with this model and the traditional real estate showing is that you don't have to pay an agent thousands of dollars to do the twenty minutes' worth of work involved.

⑦ **Make a match:** After a prospective buyer sees the home and agrees to the price, a match is officially made and the negotiation process begins. Once a match is made and good faith is established, if one of the parties backs out of the deal, the vetting system once again takes over. Any renege on the good faith agreement will result in the user's rating being severely affected, which could make it supremely difficult or challenging at best to use the system for future business.

⑧ **Execute the transaction:** After the match is made, the website will streamline the entire process. You will be connected to a network of reviewed lawyers, inspectors, title companies, and anybody else who may be required to properly execute the transaction. Agents need not apply. At the closing, we charge a fee based on the services we provided. It is not a percentage of the home's value. It will merely be based on how much service we actually gave you. In other words, did we provide a stager, tour concierge, photographer, and so on, or did we just provide the website for the peer-to-peer relationship to be built and the transaction executed? A fee of around 1.5 percent is our goal, but it will be charged in proportion to the amount of work involved. And it won't be even remotely close to the ballpark figure of an agent's percentage-based commission.

Everybody has a price. It doesn't matter if it's a new home you just built from the ground up, or if you've already lived there for ten years. The problem with the old way of selling real estate was that you didn't know if someone was willing to pay that price or not unless you officially listed your property and committed to an agent. Now, with EasyKnock and technologies like it, you will be able to know if someone out there finds your home so completely irresistible, for whatever reason, that he is compelled to *make you an offer you can't refuse.*

It's a FSBO-based model without the harassment of constant agent solicitation. If any agents contact you through our portal, let us know, and we will revoke their login credentials and never allow them access again. It's that simple. In fact, you may not even have to let us know because we may be on the lookout for this sort of disingenuous action.

THE NEW AND IMPROVED WAY
TO BUY REAL ESTATE

① **Search for free:** As a prospective buyer, you will be able to use our database to search for homes in the area of your choice for free. There's no commitment and nothing to worry about. You can use it in combination with online Mah-jongg to pass the time if you want—have fun with it!

② **Get serious, get vetted:** If after using our highly intuitive and simple user interface to search for homes, you think you've found one or two possibilities that may just be your dream home, it's time to get serious. So, you go through the quick and easy process of getting vetted. You supply all the necessary documentation, and once you are given the okay, you can bid on your potential dream home.

③ **Chat with the seller:** This can be done online or off, depending on your preferred method of communication. If you're an extremely cautious type and want a lawyer involved in this step, we can set you up with that as well.

④ **Buy your dream home:** At this point, you're able to work with the seller to schedule a time to see the home, make a match, and execute the transaction, all of which are very similar to steps six through eight on the seller's list above. You are not alone in this process. Not only are you working with the seller in a peer-to-peer manner, with no middleman to muddle transparency, but our system and the network of professionals associated with it are holding your hand the whole way.

The professionals we connect you with will also be rated, so you can be sure you're dealing with confidence and competence every step of the way. Not only will we hold your hand throughout the process, but we'll ensure that professionals who are very qualified to do the work are involved. It's not even that hard for us to do.

There are plenty of existing technologies we can tap into such as Yelp or Angie's List. We may feed into their API on the back end, or we may provide our own rating system. Either way, I guarantee it will be more transparent and trustworthy than putting your faith in the collusion of the middleman inner circle. Middlemen always have a guy they can recommend. It could be an inspector, a title guy, a mortgage guy—they always have a guy. They hand you his business card and give you a canned speech they've already used a thousand times about how great that person is, how different that person is from everybody else, and how trustworthy that person is. And one more thing: "If you mention my name, they'll give you a great deal." Don't fall into this ring of collusion. Instead, embrace the empowerment that new technology is presenting. If you use EasyKnock, great, but if you want to use another similar service, that's still better than the traditional way of spending tens of thousands of dollars for little service. Once again, *you can do this!*

ABOUT THE AUTHOR

 **JARRED KESSLER** is a vision-driven entrepreneur with over fifteen years of experience in the financial services industry, where he performed for industry stalwarts such as Morgan Stanley, Credit Suisse, and Goldman Sachs. Throughout successful endeavors with these companies, Jarred witnessed firsthand the effects of technological change on the industry. Where others failed, he became adept at evolving his career to align effectively with emerging trends. Since then, Jarred has spotted similar changes occurring in other industries. As CEO of EasyKnock, Jarred now applies this sharp awareness of change and his vision of a new and improved world to real estate.

Made in the USA
Middletown, DE
26 May 2017